Newman, Lori M.
Does advertising promote substance abuse?

DATE DUE

At Issue

Does Advertising Promote Substance Abuse?

Lori M. Newman, *Book Editor*

Bruce Glassman, *Vice President*
Bonnie Szumski, *Publisher*
Helen Cothran, *Managing Editor*

GREENHAVEN PRESS
An imprint of Thomson Gale, a part of The Thomson Corporation

THOMSON
GALE

Detroit • New York • San Francisco • San Diego • New Haven, Conn.
Waterville, Maine • London • Munich

THOMSON
GALE

For more information, contact
Greenhaven Press
27500 Drake Rd.
Farmington Hills, MI 48331-3535
Or you can visit our Internet site at http://www.gale.com

LIBRARY OF CONGRESS CATALOGING-IN-PUBLICATION DATA

Does advertising promote substance abuse? / Lori M. Newman, book editor.
p. cm. — (At issue)
Includes bibliographical references and index.
ISBN 0-7377-2364-5 (lib. : alk. paper) — ISBN 0-7377-2365-3 (pbk. : alk. paper)
1. Youth—Alcohol abuse—United States. 2. Youth—Tobacco use—United States. 3. Advertising—Alcoholic beverages—United States. 4. Advertising—Tobacco—United States. 5. Advertising and youth—United States. 6. Young consumers—United States. 7. Smoking in motion pictures. I. Newman, Lori M. II. At issue (San Diego, Calif.)
HV5135.D54 2005
616.86'1'00973—dc22 2004060653

Printed in the United States of America

Contents

Introduction

Every year companies spend billions of dollars to advertise and promote their products. They place ads on television, radio, billboards, and the Internet in an effort to persuade consumers to buy their brands. Tobacco and alcohol are among the most heavily marketed products in America. The tobacco industry spends more than $10 billion annually on advertising, and alcohol companies spend nearly $6 billion each year to promote beer, wine, and liquor. Some experts contend that much of this advertising targets young adults, contributing to increased substance abuse by minors. However, others argue that advertisements do not directly affect people's behavior and therefore do not cause young people to begin to smoke cigarettes or drink alcohol.

Some researchers argue that advertising influences young people to use and abuse tobacco and alcohol by portraying these products as sexy, grown-up, and cool. For example, alcohol companies over the years have hired celebrities, including basketball star Magic Johnson, gangsta rap singer Snoop Doggy Dogg, and NASCAR driver Dale Earnhardt Jr., to promote their alcoholic beverages. These researchers also argue that alcohol advertisers are taking advantage of the popularity of the Internet among teenagers to promote their products to young people. The Center on Alcohol Marketing and Youth (CAMY) studied the Web sites operated by seventy-four alcohol companies and found they contained many features that would attract young users, including interactive games such as car races and digital football, cartoons, chat rooms, and downloads for screensavers that contained alcohol company logos and advertising. For instance, the Amstel Light Web site offered a screensaver of characters on a beach drinking beer. According to CAMY's study, young people are being drawn to these Web sites: In the last six months of 2003 alone, about 700,000 visits to the alcohol Web sites were made by underage persons.

Other studies have reported that the many alcohol ads targeting teenagers lead to underage drinking. In a federally funded study, advertising researcher Joel Grube found that when young people are exposed to alcohol advertisements, they are more likely to drink. Grube also conducted a study of twelve-year-olds showing that those children who were more aware of beer advertising had a more positive view of drinking than did youths who had less exposure to the ads.

Critics of tobacco advertising similarly argue that ads promoting smoking as the key to popularity and upward mobility cause young people to take up smoking. According to the Campaign for Tobacco Free Kids, one-third of young people who experiment with smoking are directly influenced by tobacco advertising. The campaign also argues that cigarette marketing plays a greater role than peer pressure in causing teenagers to try smoking. One of the advertising campaigns that they criticize is Brown and Williamson's Tobacco Company's 2004 promotion of its Kool Mixx cigarettes. Ads for the product depicted images of hip hop musicians, disc jockeys, and dancers. Brown and Williamson also sponsored giveaways of Kool Mixx CD-ROMs, bags, radios, and lighters. "The themes, images, radio giveaways and music involved in the [Kool Mixx] campaign all clearly have tremendous appeal to youth, especially African-American youth," the campaign contends. In June 2004 the New York Supreme Court ruled to severely limit Brown and Williamson's advertising campaign. Now the corporation is being criticized for its candy-flavored cigarettes, including "mocha taboo" and "mintrigue," which critics argue encourage teen smoking.

Other experts counter that alcohol and tobacco advertising are not responsible for teen use of these substances. In addressing the issue of alcohol advertising, Robert A. Levy, a senior fellow at the Cato Institute, argues, "There is little evidence of any connection between . . . [alcohol] ads and underage drinking." He cites various studies finding that alcohol advertising does not increase consumption. One such study was carried out by the University of Texas over a twenty-one year period. The researchers found that the amount of money that alcohol companies spent on advertising had little effect on total consumption. Levy points to the Federal Trade Commission's 2003 Report on Alcohol Marketing and Advertising, which analyzed the marketing and advertising campaigns of nine major alcohol companies. According to the report, there is no evidence that beer and distilled spirit companies are targeting underage consumers. Furthermore, Levy notes, "The purpose of ads for alcoholic beverages, like ads for automobiles, is to encourage brand shifting, not to convert nondrinkers into drinkers."

Levy and other commentators contend that it is wrong to blame advertising as the cause of behaviors such as smoking and drinking. Young people are responsible for making their own decisions about whether or not to engage in potentially dangerous activities. Steven Milloy, the author of *Junk Science Judo: The Self-Defense Against Health Scares and Scams,* criticizes the personal injury lawyers who are filing lawsuits in many states against alcohol companies whose alcohol advertisements, they claim, have led underage consumers to drink and harm themselves or others. Milloy contends that such lawsuits "boil down to teenagers who know perfectly well they are breaking the law and lawyers who are looking for someone else to blame . . . and to pay."

John E. Calfee, a scholar at American Enterprise Institute who studies advertising, tobacco, and the tort liability system, also points out that numerous statistical analyses have failed to prove that advertising causes teenagers to start smoking. "Tell a teenager that advertising is the reason he smokes, and you will probably convince a teenager that you are out of touch with reality," Calfee states. He argues that the only way to discourage teen smoking is to encourage young people to have a sense of personal accountability for their decisions and health.

The debate over the influence of advertising on young people's behavior is likely to continue well into the future. The authors in *At Issue: Does Advertising Promote Substance Abuse?* present many views on this continuing controversy.

1

Alcohol Advertising Targets Youths

Global Alcohol Policy Alliance

The Global Alcohol Policy Alliance's stated mission is "to reduce alcohol-related harm worldwide by promoting science-based policies independent of commercial interests." It achieves this mission by creating a forum for alcohol policy advocates to discuss alcohol-related issues, drawing the attention of lawmakers and advocates to these issues, disseminating information on alcohol policy and advocacy, encouraging research on the effects of the alcoholic beverage industry, and monitoring industry activities.

Fruit-flavored alcoholic beverages called "alcopops" specifically target the youth market. George Hacker of the Center for Science in the Public Interest (CSPI) calls these beverages gateway drugs that lure young people into drinking and prepare them for alcohol consumption as adults. A poll conducted by CSPI showed that 41 percent of teens had tried alcopops and preferred these beverages to beer and mixed drinks. In addition, 90 percent of teens said that trying alcopops would make them more likely to try other kinds of alcoholic beverages. Because alcohol causes so much harm to young people, CSPI has mounted a powerful media campaign to fight the marketing of alcohol to young people.

Several years after they appeared in Europe, alcopops [sweet alcoholic beverages tasting similar to soda] have reached the United States. Their appearance coincided with the time of the year when teenagers attend prom and graduation parties—traditions familiar to anyone who has seen any of the countless "rite of passage" films produced over the years. Critics of the booze industry recognise an attempt to ensure that these young people, as they move from school to college, growing from adolescence to adulthood, are recruited to the ranks of regular drinkers. . . .

> *"Booze merchants formulate the products and the design of their labelling and packaging specifically to appeal to people who don't like the taste of alcohol, which includes teenagers."*

The drink industry was accused of aiming these sweet, fruit-flavoured drinks at the teenage market. It was a way, the argument went, of accustoming young people to the consumption of alcohol when they might otherwise find the taste of conventional drinks—beer, distilled spirits—unpleasant. The same reaction has met their launch in the United States. The Center for Science in the Public Interest (CSPI) commissioned a poll to assess the public perception of alcopops. Unsurprisingly, the findings show that they appeal more to teenagers than the adult market for which the producers claim they are intended and that these same young people are more likely to drink them.

Pulling no punches, George Hacker, CSPI's director of alcohol policies, told a press conference in Washington that "booze merchants formulate the products and the design of their labelling and packaging specifically to appeal to people who don't like the taste of alcohol, which includes teenagers. Alcopops are gateway drugs that ease young people into drinking and pave the way to more traditional beverages."

Poll Shows the Serious Impact of Alcopops

In the poll, by a margin of three to one, teenagers showed a greater familiarity with alcopops than adults, and seventeen and eighteen year olds were more than twice as likely to have drunk them. [A] majority of both adults and teenagers polled believed that alcopops were aimed at people below the legal age of purchase, which in the United States is twenty-one. There was an overwhelming opinion that alcopops were made to taste like lemonade in order to lure young people into trying them: 90 per cent of teenagers and 67 per cent of adults took this view.

The poll also showed that:

- 41 per cent of teenagers had tried alcopops;
- 90 per cent of teenagers agreed that drinking these new, sweeter drinks would make it more likely that they would try other alcoholic beverages;
- twice as many 14 to 16 year olds preferred them to beer or mixed drinks;
- more than half of all the teenagers questioned pointed to attributes of the products—their sweet taste, the disguised taste of alcohol, and their easy-to-drink character—as major reasons why they would choose them in preference to beer, wine, or cocktails.

Hacker has no doubt about the motivation of the drink industry: "Companies that market "starter brews" and alcopops aren't peddling adult drinks. Those alcopop drinks can have serious implications for America's youth and for alcohol-related problems throughout society." It has been shown in many studies that early onset of drinking means a greater likelihood of problems later in life. George Hacker quoted a study by the National Institute on Alcohol Abuse and Alcoholism which indicated young people who begin drinking before the age of fifteen are four times more likely to develop alcohol dependency that those who delay starting until they are aged twenty-one.

Research shows that ten million Americans between the ages of twelve and twenty drink alcohol and, according to CSPI, it kills more teenagers than all the illegal drugs combined. In addition, the Center says that alcohol is a major factor in the four main causes of death among teenagers—car accidents, unintentional injuries, homicides, and suicides. Figures calculated for the U.S. Department of Justice show that underage drinking cost the nation something on the order of $53 billion in 1996 alone.

CSPI Fights Alcopops Effectively

The CSPI's alcopop campaign is a model of successful advocacy. The Globe asked George Hacker [how] it was done:

From the very beginning, says Hacker, we planned our efforts to maximize the potential for media exposure. Even in advance of our research activities, we "pitched" the story (alcopops' appeal to underage persons) to a number of television and print outlets, and, as a result received early coverage in *Newsweek* that brought credibility (and other reporters) to the issue. By hooking up, early on, and working closely with a popular television news magazine for a lengthier feature story we were able to educate the producers and frame the issue on our terms.

We also took care to: audio- and videotape our focus groups of teenagers (who, unaided, said brilliantly provocative things about alcopops) for later use in the media; create strong visuals and [a] solid press package that would slice through ordinary news clutter. We recruited a U.S. Congressman and several strong, representative youth-advocacy and alcoholism organisations as allies at the press-conference, and even sponsored taste tests for reporters of several brands of alcopops to demonstrate how much like soft drinks, as opposed to alcohol, they tasted.

In addition, our press materials provocatively reported a national poll (by a prominent polling firm) that demonstrated the new alcopop drinks "lured" teens to alcohol. We dubbed them "starter suds." In those materials, we also announced demands that the appropriate government agencies investigate and do something about the new teen-oriented concoctions. In anticipation of our press event, we left few stones unturned, and aggressively promoted the story to television networks. Fortuitously, our press conference coincided, generally, with the introduction of the first television [ads] for Mike's Hard Lemonade, one of the more popular brands. Their off-beat presentations also received some coverage.

CSPI's alcopops' campaign will continue as one element in our efforts to combat alcohol marketing to young people. In particular, this issue provides strong evidence of the need for a national media campaign to counter underage drinking, another measure we have been promoting among national law makers.

2

Alcohol Advertising Does Not Target Youths

Federal Trade Commission

The Federal Trade Commission (FTC) aims to ensure that the nation's markets run efficiently and without restrictions that harm consumers. It also enforces federal consumer protection and antitrust laws to protect consumers. In addition, the FTC performs economic research and analysis to support its law enforcement work and to contribute to policy development.

Given the risks posed by underage drinking, it is important to carefully examine the influence of alcohol marketing on youth audiences. The Federal Trade Commission examined the advertising of flavored malt beverages (FMBs), a relatively new alcoholic product containing fruit or cola flavors, in order to see if companies were targeting minors. After studying alcohol company advertising displays and internal documents regarding marketing practices, the Federal Trade Commission determined that FMBs are marketed to adults of legal drinking age. These products are placed in displays containing other alcoholic drinks, rather than colas or juices, and are generally not advertised during television programs that have primarily youth audiences. In addition, the majority of FMB consumers are over age twenty-seven. Evidence regarding the impact of FMB advertising on minors was inconclusive, but this does not obviate the need for alcohol producers to exercise great caution in marketing their products.

Federal Trade Commission, "Alcohol Marketing and Advertising: A Report to Congress," www.ftc.gov, September 2003.

Concerns about the marketing of alcohol reflect the serious costs of underage alcohol use. Underage drinking has declined significantly since all states adopted 21 as the minimum legal drinking age two decades ago, but drinking by minors remains high. In 2002, one-fifth of 8th graders, over one-third of 10th graders, and nearly half of 12th graders reported drinking within the past 30 days, and significant numbers reported engaging in binge drinking.

The manner in which minors drink places them at risk of significant harm. Excessive drinking is associated with a variety of risky behaviors and injury, including drunk driving accidents, suicide, sexual assault, and high-risk sexual activity. Public health organizations, the government, and the alcohol industry have all recognized that it is important to reduce underage drinking in order to lessen drinking-related harm.

Given the risks of underage drinking, all involved agree that the alcohol industry advertising must avoid targeting minors.

Marketing Flavored Malt Beverages

In recent years, flavored malt beverages (FMBs) have become increasingly popular. These products combine beer and distilled spirits characteristics. To produce a FMB, a brewer starts with a base of beer, uses filtering techniques to remove a portion of the

Figure 1: Long-Term Trends in Use of Alcohol for 8th, 10th, and 12th Graders
(Students reporting one or more drinks in the past month)

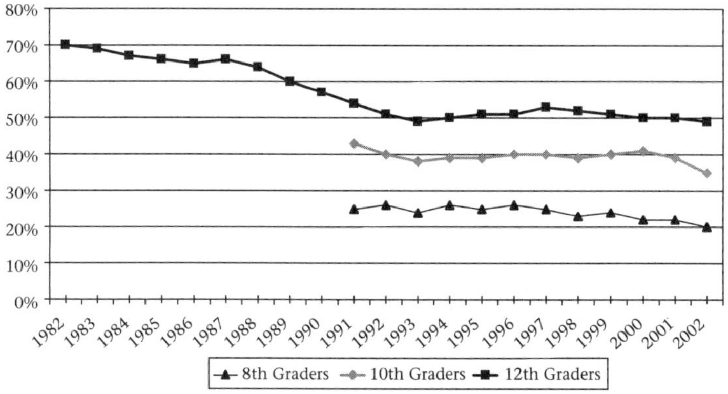

The Monitoring the Future Study, the University of Michigan.

beer taste, and adds flavors derived from spirits to achieve the desired taste and alcohol level. FMBs are marketed in traditional beer bottles, and have an alcohol content of 4% to 6% by volume, similar to other beers.

Marketers introduced citrus-flavored FMBs, including "hard" lemonades in the late 1990's. More recently, brewers have entered into agreements with distillers to introduce spirits-branded FMBs that typically taste like a combination of light beer and citrus or other fruit. Other FMBs have flavors similar to wine coolers or cocktails (such as bourbon and cola).

> *"On a few occasions, FMB ads appeared on individual episodes of teen-themed shows in individual TV markets in 2002. Given the high overall compliance, however, these incidents appeared to have been inadvertent, rather than deliberate attempts to target teens."*

FMBs are relatively new products. As a result of efforts to introduce them into the marketplace, a disproportionate share of beer advertising expenditures currently are directed to FMBs. As new products have been introduced [since the late 1990's] these expenditures have increased dramatically, from 2% of beer advertising in 1998 to approximately 17% of beer advertising in 2002. During that same period of time, FMB sales grew at a far slower pace, from 1.3% of beer sales in 1998 to approximately 3% of beer sales in 2002. Over this time, total per capita beer consumption has increased modestly, by about 1% per annum; a substantial portion of FMB sales are derived from consumers who have reduced purchases of other malt beverages.

2001 Report Finds Youths Not Targeted

In 2001, in response to a complaint filed by the Center for Science in the Public Interest (CSPI), the FTC conducted an investigation to determine if FMBs were being targeted to minors. Among other things, the Commission staff reviewed whether the products were placed among non-alcoholic beverages in retail outlets; whether the advertising for these newer products was targeted to an underage audience; and whether consumer survey evidence proved that teens were more likely than adults to be aware of and use the products, as alleged in the CSPI complaint. . . .

With respect to the placement of FMBs in retail outlets, industry documents obtained by the FTC showed that the alcohol companies had expressly urged distributors to place the products with other alcohol products, generally with imports and microbrews. The survey of retail outlets in ten cities confirmed that the beverages were not co-mingled with non-alcoholic products in retail outlets.

The Commission's review also found no evidence of intent to target minors with the FMB products, packaging, or advertising. For example, the internal company documentation, including planning materials and consumer research results, demonstrated that the marketers tested alternate product and packaging versions on adults aged 21 to 29 to determine the optimal product taste profiles and packaging styles and that they tested the appeal of advertising by surveying adults above the legal drinking age.

Finally, the Commission reviewed the consumer survey evidence submitted in support of the proposition that the new malt beverages are predominantly popular with minors. The Commission concluded that flaws in the survey's methodology limit the ability to draw conclusions from the survey data.

Ads Absent from Youth Television

In response to [a] March 2003 request, the Commission initiated a new review of the advertising and marketing of FMBs. The Commission sent compulsory process requests to nine alcohol industry members, eight of whom market one or more beverages that compete in the FMB category. The compulsory process requests required the companies to produce internal documents relating to the marketing of these products, including documents describing the target audiences and relating to advertising development and placement.

The Commission obtained marketing plans discussing the advertisement placement strategies for the FMBs as well as data showing the age composition of the audience for FMB ads. In 2002 the industry codes required that at least 50% of the audience for alcohol advertising consist of adults aged 21 and over. The Commission's review shows that, in 2002, over 99% of the dollars spent to advertise FMBs on television, radio, and in print media were expended in compliance with this goal.

Although compliance with the 50% standard was quite high, the standard still permitted ads to be placed in venues with a substantial underage audience composition. To limit the likelihood that ads for FMBs (or other alcohol) would appear in such venues, five companies also maintained lists of programs on which they would not place ads ("no buy" lists). Typically, they instructed their media buyers not to place ads on MTV or the UPN network, on wrestling or extreme sports shows, or on teen-oriented shows such as "Malcolm in the Middle," "Gilmore Girls," "Boston Public," "Sabrina," "Grounded for Life," "Celebrity Death Match," "Dawson's Creek," "Moesha," "7th Heaven," and "Popular." A sixth company limited the likelihood of placement on teen-oriented shows by requiring a 70% adult audience for placements. Finally, two of the companies marketing FMBs did not advertise their products in print or broadcast media.

"The documents provided by the companies indicate that marketing for FMBs is targeted to adults 21 and over; that companies measure product success in terms of use by adults; and that adults in fact use the products."

The companies' documents showed that on a few occasions, FMB ads appeared on individual episodes of teen-theme shows in individual TV markets in 2002. Given the high overall compliance, however, these incidents appeared to have been inadvertent, rather than deliberate attempts to target teens.

Ad Content for Adults

The alcohol company documents submitted . . . indicate that the companies target advertising for the FMBs to persons of legal drinking age and older. Marketing concepts (including advertising and packaging) are directed to a specific "target" category of consumers. The company documents show that the intended targets for FMBs were above the legal drinking age, generally 21-year-olds to 27- or 29-year-olds.

The companies' documents further indicate that before ads

are disseminated, the alcohol companies often use consumer research to test them for persuasiveness and efficacy. Research participants are screened for target demographic characteristics including age, generally 21 to 29, and are asked a wide range of questions, including questions designed to elicit whether the ad is appealing and whether it communicates that the advertised brand appeals to the target.

Further, industry-conducted research on consumers over the age of 21 who use FMBs shows that these consumers generally view the FMBs as substitutes for beer, although companies developed them in part to attract consumers who did not like beer's taste (often women). The research indicates that adult FMB drinkers see the brands as appropriate for use on a wide variety of occasions where they consume alcohol. This research also concludes that consumers are not likely to consume more than two or three FMBs on any occasion because of the products' sweetness.

To evaluate the success of FMB sales, the industry members rely on survey information about product awareness, trial, and repeat usage among consumers aged 21 to 27, and among older segments. These data show that in 2002, FMBs had substantial sales to adults. Although consumers who are 21 to 27 are the largest single group of FMB users, the majority of FMB drinkers are over the age of 27:

21–27	41%
28–34	22%
35–49	26%
50+	11%

These data also show that users of FMBs are somewhat more likely to be female, a fact which industry attributes to the products sweeter taste.

In summary, the documents provided by the companies indicate that marketing for FMBs is targeted to adults 21 and over; that companies measure product success in terms of use by adults; and that adults in fact use the products.

Questionable Effect on Minors

The Commission [also looked] at the impact on underage consumers of the expansion of marketing for FMBs. As noted in the 1999 Report, advertising campaigns targeted to 21-year-olds may also appeal to those under 21. Thus, the companies' advertising for FMBs may have had a "spillover" effect on teens, and the products' sweeter tastes seem likely to appeal to teens. The company documents and other evidence available to the Commission did not provide information on the particular impact on minors of this expanded marketing. There also are no reliable survey data on the brands that teens drink and thus there are no data on whether or how many teens drink FMBs, or the impact of FMB advertising on such drinking. The available data show that, despite increases in FMB advertising, overall drinking by minors decreased between 2000 and 2002. . . . In any event, given that many factors influence teen drinking, including individual, family, peer, and environmental factors, it is not clear that changes in drinking trends can be attributed to changes in advertising.

Ads OK, but Caution Necessary

The Commission's investigation of the marketing, sale, and use of FMBs indicates that adults 21 to 29 appear to be the intended target of FMB marketing; that the products have established a niche in the adult market; and that FMB ads were placed in compliance with the industry's 50% placement standard. At the same time, the 50% placement standard in effect when these products were introduced permitted the ads to reach a substantial youth audience. Further, some themes attractive to new legal drinkers, as well as the products' sweet tastes, may also be attractive to minors. Although it is probable that some teens drink FMBs, teen drinking continued to decline during the period when these beverages were being aggressively marketed.

The Commission believes, nonetheless, that marketers should exercise strong caution when introducing new alcohol products, to ensure that they are not directed to an underage audience. Further, the Commission continues to recommend that labels for all beverage alcohol products, including FMBs, be required to disclose accurately the alcohol content by volume.

3

Alcohol Advertising Contributes to Teen Alcohol Abuse

Jean Kilbourne

Jean Kilbourne is a world-renowned researcher, writer, filmmaker, and speaker on the effects of alcohol and tobacco advertising on girls and women. She is the author of several books, including Can't Buy My Love: How Advertising Changes the Way We Think and Feel. *Her film titles include* Spin the Bottle: Sex, Lies, and Alcohol *and* Pack of Lies: The Advertising of Tobacco.

Although no one has demonstrated that advertising directly increases alcohol consumption and abuse, it is clear that there is a link. The alcohol industry targets heavy drinkers in its advertising because they are the most lucrative consumers; however, young people are also a target because they are potential consumers of alcohol products. Many alcohol ads portray drinking as a rite of passage, even as the number of teen drunk-driving fatalities remain extremely high. Alcohol use is also a factor in many of the other major causes of death of minors, including suicides, homicides, and accidents. In all its efforts to promote "moderate" youth drinking, the alcohol industry fails to present abstinence as an option. In addition, alcohol advertising suggests that excessive consumption is the norm and that alcohol improves many aspects of life. Society desperately needs to regulate alcohol and nicotine products and advertising.

Jean Kilbourne, "Targets of Alcohol Advertising," www.health20-20.org, 2000.

Alcohol is the most commonly used drug in the United States. It is also one of the most heavily advertised products in the United States. The alcohol industry generates more than $65 billion a year in revenue and spends more than $1 billion a year on advertising. The advertising budget for one beer—Budweiser—is more than the entire federal budget for research on alcoholism and alcohol use. Unfortunately, young people and heavy drinkers are the primary targets of the advertisers.

There is no conclusive proof that advertising increases alcohol consumption. Research does indicate, however, that alcohol advertising contributes to increases in consumption by young people and serves as a significant source of negative socialization for young people. Those who argue that peer pressure is a major influence on young people strangely overlook the role of advertising.

The alcoholic beverage companies claim that they are not trying to create more or heavier drinkers. They say that they only want people who already drink to switch to another brand and that they want them to drink the new brand in moderation. But this industry-wide claim does not hold up under scrutiny. An editorial in *Advertising Age* concluded: "A strange world it is, in which people spending millions on advertising must do their best to prove that advertising doesn't do very much!"

Advertising Promotes Heavy Drinking

About a third of Americans choose not to drink at all, a third drink moderately, and about a third drink regularly. Ten percent of the drinking age population consumes over 60 percent of the alcohol. This figure corresponds closely to the percentage of alcoholics in society. If alcoholics were to recover (i.e., to stop drinking entirely), the alcohol industry's gross revenues would be cut in half.

Recognizing this important marketing fact, alcohol companies deliberately devise ads designed to appeal to heavy drinkers. Advertising is usually directed toward promoting loyalty and increasing usage, and heavy users of any product are the best customers. The heavy user of alcohol is usually an addict.

Another perspective on the industry's claim that it encourages only moderate drinking is provided by Robert Hammond, director of the Alcohol Research Information Service. He estimates that if all 105 million drinkers of legal age in the US consumed the official maximum "moderate" amount of alcohol,

.99 ounces per day, the equivalent of about two drinks, the industry would suffer "a whopping 40 percent decrease in the sale of beer, wine and distilled spirits, based on 1981 sales figures."

Such statistics show the role heavy drinkers play in maintaining the large profit margins of the alcohol industry. Modern research techniques allow the producers of print and electronic media to provide advertisers with detailed information about their readers, listeners, and viewers. Target audiences are sold to the alcohol industry on a cost per drinker basis.

One example of how magazines sell target audiences appeared recently in *Advertising Age: Good Housekeeping* advertised itself to the alcohol industry as a good place to reach women drinkers, proclaiming "You'll catch more women with wine than with vinegar. She's a tougher customer than ever. You never needed *Good Housekeeping* more."

Ads Target Youths

The young audience is also worth a great deal to the alcohol industry. *Sport* magazine promoted itself to the alcohol industry as a conduit to young drinkers with an ad in *Advertising Age* stating, "What young money spends on drinks is a real eye-opener."

Social learning theory suggests that repeated exposure to modeled behavior can result in behavioral change. The impact of modeling on young people is particularly important given the widespread use of such celebrities as rock stars, television personalities, and athletes in alcohol ads. Alcohol ads feature only very healthy, attractive, and youthful-looking people. Advertising is a powerful educational force in American culture, one that promotes attitudes and values as well as products.

The "Seventh Special Report to the US Congress on Alcohol and Health" [by the U.S. Department of Health and Human Services] found evidence that early positive expectations about alcohol were strong predictors of drinking behavior in adolescence. "Children at highest risk were most likely to have strong expectancies of social enhancement and to believe that alcohol improves cognitive and motor functioning."

What more powerful source of these early expectancies is there in a culture than alcohol advertising? Indeed, one of the functions of advertising is to induce these early expectancies. According to an editorial in *Advertising Age*, "Quite clearly, the company that has not bothered to create a favorable attitude toward its product before the potential customer goes shopping hasn't much of a chance of snaring the bulk of potential buyers."

No wonder ads feature characters with special appeal to children. The Spuds MacKenzie figure reportedly has been licensed by Anheuser-Busch to the makers of some 200 consumer products, including stuffed animals, dolls, T-shirts, posters, and mugs. In one Christmas ad campaign, Spuds appeared in a Santa Claus suit, promoting 12-packs of Bud Light beer. In another ad he is cavorting with ninjas, drawing on the popularity of the Teenage Mutant Ninja Turtles movie. "Heavy Metal," proclaims one Budweiser ad featuring a six-pack—hardly an ad designed for the middle-aged crowd.

Drinking as a Rite of Passage

Many alcohol ads play on the theme that drinking is the primary ritual into adulthood in our society. Others turn soft drinks into alcoholic drinks, often in a way that scoffs at the idea of a soft drink standing alone (e.g., an ad for a wine cooler says, "Sick of soft drinks? Here's thirst aid"). Even in supposedly commercial-free movies showing in theaters, viewers are targeted. Many films, especially those appealing to young people, include paid placements of cigarettes and alcohol.

The average age at which people begin drinking today is 12. A *Weekly Reader* survey found that more than one-third of fourth graders surveyed had experienced peer pressure to drink alcohol. A 1988 survey of high-school seniors found that 92 percent had used alcohol (while 54 percent had used another illegal drug). At least three of 10 adolescents have alcohol problems.

> *"Research does indicate . . . that alcohol advertising contributes to increases in consumption by young people and serves as a significant source of negative socialization for young people."*

Youthful drinking is frequently characterized by heavy binge drinking, making youngsters a lucrative market for alcohol producers. According to the 1989 National Institute on Drug Abuse survey of high-school seniors, 33 percent reported they had consumed five or more drinks on one occasion within the previous two weeks.

More than 40 percent of teenage deaths are caused by motor vehicle crashes. More than half of those are alcohol related. Alcohol is implicated in at least half of the other major causes of death for young people, i.e., suicides, homicides, and accidents. Alcohol use is often a factor in many of the other problems afflicting this age group, such as teenage pregnancy, date rape, suicide, assault, and vandalism.

The college market is particularly important to the alcohol industry not only because of the money the students will spend on beer today, but because they may develop drinking habits and brand allegiances for a lifetime. As one marketing executive said, "Let's not forget that getting a freshman to choose a certain brand of beer may mean that he will maintain his brand loyalty for the next 20 to 35 years. If he turns out to be a big drinker, the beer company has bought itself an annuity." This statement undercuts the industry's claim that it does not target advertising campaigns at underage drinkers since today almost every state prohibits the sale of alcohol to people under 21 years old and the vast majority of college freshmen are below that age.

Encouraging "Moderation" over Abstinence

The alcohol industry's efforts to promote responsible drinking must also be evaluated carefully. Much of its advertising promotes irresponsible and dangerous drinking. For example, a poster for Pabst Blue Ribbon features a young woman speeding along on a bicycle with a bottle of beer where the water bottle is supposed to be. Obviously biking and drinking beer are not safely complementary activities.

Even some of the programs designed by the alcohol industry to educate students about responsible drinking subtly promote myths and damaging attitudes. Budweiser has a program called "The Buddy System," designed to encourage young people not to let their friends drive drunk. Although this is a laudable goal, it is interesting to note that none of the alcohol industry programs discourage or even question drunkenness per se. The implicit message is that it is acceptable to get drunk as long as you don't drive.

The alcohol industry programs do not offer abstinence as a possible choice. Miller's [2000] "moderation" slogan is "Think when you drink." This is particularly ironic, given that the ability to think clearly is one of the first things affected by alcohol. Miller also has a campus alcohol education program that defines moderate drinking as four drinks a day (heavy drinking by any standards).

The [2000] Budweiser "moderation" campaign says, "Know when to say when," as opposed to "Know when to say no." In the guise of a moderation message, this slogan actually suggests to young people that drinking beer is one way to demonstrate their control. It also perpetuates the myth that alcoholics are simply people who are irresponsibly engaging in willful misconduct, rather than people who are suffering from a disease that afflicts at least one in 10 drinkers. "Know when to say when" is purposefully vague and misleading. . . .

Advertising Promotes Distorted Images

The link between advertising and alcoholism is unproven. Alcoholism is a complex illness and its etiology is uncertain. But alcohol advertising does create a climate in which abusive attitudes toward alcohol are presented as normal, appropriate, and innocuous. One of the chief symptoms of alcoholism is denial that there is a problem. It is often not only the alcoholic who denies the illness but also his or her family, employer, doctor, etc. Alcohol advertising often encourages denial by creating a world in which myths about alcohol are presented as true and in which signs of trouble are erased or transformed into positive attributes.

One of the primary means of creating this distortion is through advertising. Most advertising is essentially mythmaking. Instead of providing information about a product, such as its taste or quality, advertisements create an image of the product, linking the item with a particular lifestyle which may have little or nothing to do with the product itself. According to an article on beer marketing in *Advertising Age*, "Advertising is as important to selling beer as the bottle opener is to drinking it. . . . Beer advertising is mainly an exercise in building images." Another article a few months later on liquor marketing stated that "product image is probably the most important element in selling liquor. The trick for marketers is to project the right message in their advertisements to motivate those motionless consumers to march down to the liquor store or bar and exchange their money for a sip of image."

The links are generally false and arbitrary but we are so surrounded by them that we come to accept them: the jeans will make you look sexy, the car will give you confidence, the detergent will save your marriage. Advertising spuriously links alcohol with precisely those attributes and qualities—happiness, wealth, prestige, sophistication, success, maturity, athletic ability, virility, creativity, sexual satisfaction, and others—that the use of alcohol destroys. For example, alcohol is often linked with romance and sexual fulfillment, yet it is common knowledge that alcohol use can lead to sexual dysfunction. Less well known is the fact that heavy drinkers and alcoholics are seven times more likely than the general population to be separated or divorced.

> *"Advertising spuriously links alcohol with precisely those attributes and qualities—happiness, wealth, prestige, sophistication, success, maturity, athletic ability, virility, creativity, sexual satisfaction, and others—that the use of alcohol destroys."*

Image advertising is especially appealing to young people, who are more likely than adults to be insecure about the image they are projecting. Sexual and athletic prowess are two of the themes that dominate advertising aimed at young people. A recent television commercial for Miller beer featured Danny Sullivan, the race car driver, speeding around a track with the Miller logo emblazoned everywhere. The ad implies that Miller beer and fast driving go hand in hand. A study of beer commercials funded by the American Automobile Association found that they often linked beer with images of speed, including speeding cars. . . .

Addressing the Problem

Western culture as a whole, not just the advertising and alcohol industry, tends to glorify alcohol and dismiss the problems associated with it. The "war on drugs," as covered by newspapers and magazines in this country, rarely includes the two major killers, alcohol and nicotine. It is no coincidence that these are two of the most heavily advertised products. In 1987 the use of all illegal drugs combined accounted for about 3,400 deaths. Alcohol is linked with over 100,000 deaths annually. Cigarettes kill a thousand people every day.

A comprehensive effort is needed to prevent alcohol-related problems. Such an effort must include education, media campaigns, increased availability of treatment programs and more effective deterrence policies. It must also include public policy changes that would include raising taxes on alcohol, putting clearly legible warning labels on the bottles, and regulating the advertising.

The kind of public education essential to solving our major drug problem is probably not possible until the media no longer depend on the goodwill of the alcohol industry. For this reason alone, we need some controls on alcohol. One doesn't even have to enter into the argument about whether such advertising increases consumption. At the very least, it drastically inhibits honest public discussion of the problem in the media and creates a climate in which alcohol use is seen as entirely benign.

4

Advertising Has No Effect on Alcohol and Tobacco Consumption

John E. Calfee

John E. Calfee is a resident scholar at the American Enterprise Institute for Public Policy Research (AEI), a think tank in Washington, D.C. He researches and writes about pharmaceuticals, the Food and Drug Administration, health care policy, advertising, and tobacco.

Advertising does not affect people's decisions to consume alcohol, nor does it increase the size of the alcohol market. It simply redistributes market shares among various advertisers. Similarly, tobacco advertising does not affect consumption. Lawsuits against tobacco companies and their advertising have therefore only served to raise prices of tobacco products, enriching law firms and state governments. Litigation has also reduced tobacco advertising and has made life more difficult for smokers while causing little change in the smoking rates of youths and adults.

There is quite a bit of research on the effects of alcohol advertising. This research began, roughly speaking, in the mid-1970s. Economists have studied the effects of alcohol advertising in the United States, the United Kingdom and various European countries. There are now dozens of such studies. They have employed a large variety of econometric models and diverse data sets. . . .

No Evidence Advertising Affects Consumption

Invariably, empirical research finds no effect of advertising on the total amount of alcohol consumption. Yet this is precisely where the effects of advertising should be the easiest to detect. When advertising goes up by 10 percent, 50 percent, or 200 percent, as sometimes happens, you ought to be able to find at least a measurable blip in total consumption—assuming, of course, that advertising really does affect consumption. But those blips cannot be found.

This is true even in places like France and the Netherlands, which I've studied myself and which have provided remarkable natural experiments in the dynamics of advertising. In the Netherlands, for example, alcoholic beverage advertising doubled between 1990 and 1994, with no perceptible impact on consumption. In France, advertising tripled between 1977 and 1989, and then was almost completely banned by [law] in 1991. Alcohol consumption in France continued to decline at about the same annual rate throughout this entire period.

Why doesn't advertising have the effects that so many people seem to expect it to have? I think the intuitive answer is fairly straightforward. When it comes to something as basic as the decision of whether to drink—or whether to smoke, for that matter—advertising is a very weak force. There's almost no evidence that advertising has an impact on decisions to initiate or continue those kinds of behavior. Those decisions are deeply embedded in such matters as family environment. That's one reason for the widespread failure of social marketing campaigns in which governments use advertising to persuade people not to engage in certain behaviors such as underage drinking, smoking, illicit drug use, or unprotected sex. That kind of advertising has proved extremely difficult to pull off successfully. Using the mass media to affect those kinds of decisions is a very difficult task.

Advertising as Solely a Market Force

What advertising usually does achieve is simply to drive market shares. Economically speaking, there are perfectly rational explanations for this. Individual sellers have a strong incentive to engage in advertising. Even if it's true, as it is for alcoholic beverages, that advertising has no impact on the total market size, it does have an impact on brand shares.

Economists have been fiddling around with these ideas for

a number of years. Somewhere along the line, someone formulated what is called the "fallacy of composition." The fallacy of composition is the assumption that if a certain economic activity, such as advertising, benefits each individual participant in the market, such as manufacturers of individual brands, then all the advertising put together must benefit the entire market. This reason does not hold up in general, nor does it hold up for advertising in particular. In other words, each brand may do better when it advertises than when it doesn't advertise, but total advertising may have no effect on total sales in the market. The brand-level effects may offset each other. This is in fact what we find in alcoholic beverage markets.

"Invariably, empirical research finds no effect of advertising on the total amount of alcohol consumption."

For a good example of the fallacy of composition, look at political advertising. There is no doubt that advertising has a profound effect on individual politicians' share of the vote. But there's no evidence that political advertising increases total voter turnout. . . .

Fighting Tobacco on Weak Grounds

What we see in the case of tobacco advertising is the same thing we see with alcohol advertising. Incentives to advertise individual brands are very strong. We observe effects from advertising at the brand level, but no effects on the overall volume of smoking. And, as far as anyone has been able to document, we find no effects from advertising on youth smoking.

Nonetheless, tobacco litigation [lawsuits against tobacco companies] eventually transferred immense amounts of money, and it did so only after litigation was initiated by state governments in state courts. The state litigation finally put juries in the position where they had the power to bankrupt the defendants through a single adverse decision. That was the essence of the circumstances that generated the mass settlement agreement, which before it expires will transfer several hundred billions of dollars, mainly to state governments.

All this happened despite the fact that the premises of the tobacco litigation were highly questionable. Essentially, the tobacco litigation succeeded despite being based mainly on untenable arguments. One was that advertising causes smoking. Another was that smoking increased health care costs for state governments and private insurers; there's no evidence that that actually happened. Another allegation, which I personally think is absurd, is that the state governments and (according to the current lawsuit brought by the U.S. Department of Justice) the federal government were actually deceived into thinking that smoking really wasn't very harmful. In fact, it's perfectly obvious from the historical record, as well as from documents generated by litigation, that on the whole what governments knew about smoking and health was pretty much what the tobacco companies knew. The tobacco manufacturers were getting their information about the health effects of smoking mainly from the same sources as the public health community. The industry was engaged mainly in monitoring and replicating the publicly available medical literature. Nonetheless, the tobacco litigation has had large effects. We should pay close attention to those effects because tobacco litigation is a model for regulation by litigation generally.

> *"Smoking today is a far more difficult activity to engage in than it used to be."*

This tobacco litigation directly generated large price increases on the order of 30 to 50 percent. The increased revenues were mainly handed over to state governments. The litigation and its tax-like effects also provided some of the intellectual and political foundations for even larger legislated increases in state taxes. The litigation has also greatly reduced the volume and variety of tobacco advertising. In fact, I for one hardly ever see any tobacco ads these days.

Smoking Rates Stable Despite Advertising Changes

I think the tobacco litigation has also enhanced the political power of advocates seeking increasingly pervasive controls over smoking. Smoking today is a far more difficult activity to engage in than it used to be. It's harder to buy cigarettes and it's harder to find places to smoke them. Finally, the litigation has also generated a great deal of antismoking activity, especially in the mass media, but also in the schools and elsewhere.

Nonetheless, when you look back over the last 15 years or so at what really counts—smoking behavior itself—it's amazing how little has changed. Roughly 20 to 25 percent of the adult population smokes. That's pretty much what it was in the early 1990s. This is consistent with long-run trends in developed countries around the world. In the U.S. and Western Europe, and recently in Japan, smoking prevalence declined steadily and substantially after knowledge of smoking and its harm became better established and widely disseminated. Smoking declined most rapidly in the U.S. even though the U.S. was long the home of the most prominent and creative cigarette advertising. But when the prevalence of smoking gets down to about 20 to 25 percent of adults, it usually gets stuck. That's pretty much what's happened in the U.S. as well as elsewhere. Massive litigation has had very little impact on overall smoking rates.

Youth smoking has also changed remarkably little, although here the data are softer and less stable. In fact, youth smoking actually increased during the early 1990s. [Since 2002], the antismoking community has celebrated the fact that smoking by high school students is finally back down to where it was before all this litigation began.

5

Alcohol Advertisements on Race Cars Promote Underage Drinking

Steve Wilstein

Steve Wilstein is a longtime sportswriter and columnist for the Associated Press. He is the author of The Associated Press Sports Writing Handbook.

In the fall of 2004, NASCAR (the National Association for Stock Car Auto Racing) decided to permit hard-liquor advertisements on race cars. This decision is dangerous. While many NASCAR fans are adults, young people constitute a significant segment of the fan base. These ads will cause young fans to associate drinking with "life in the fast lane" and lead them to conclude that drinking and driving is an acceptable behavior. While the alcohol industry claims its ads will promote responsible drinking behavior, ads on race cars will only encourage underage drinking.

Mixed messages, like too many mixed cocktails, can cause a nasty hangover.

NASCAR is setting itself up for a lulu of a head-splitter by trying to reconcile hard-liquor ads on race cars with efforts to spiff up the image of a sport that traces its roots to moonshine runners.

It's kind of schizo-marketing to extol a wholesome "family values" business while drivers are behind the wheels of speed-

Steve Wilstein, "NASCAR's Liquor Ads Are a Bad Idea," http://msnbc.msn.com, November 13, 2004.

ing cars painted like beer cans and, soon, Jack Daniel's and other whiskey bottles.

In NASCAR's world, where the name of the game is sponsorship, drinking and driving go together a little too neatly. . . .

On one level, the [November 2004] decision to lift the ban on hard-liquor ads is no big deal. Budweiser sponsors [NASCAR driver Dale] Earnhardt [Jr.'s] car, [pro racer] Matt Kenseth has a deal with Smirnoff ICE malt beverage, and Busch sponsors a whole lower-tier racing series. There's enough beer poured by fans at a race to float all the cars.

Sending Mixed Messages

So why should anyone get worked up over letting the drivers hawk higher-proof booze? Whiskey, beer, wine? It's all alcohol and it's all legal, unlike the moonshine that the good ol' boys barreled through the hills of Georgia and the Carolinas way back when.

Let's not cry out for a return to Prohibition but let's not kid ourselves that a sport like NASCAR, and the sponsorships behind it, doesn't influence its fans, young and old.

Let's not pretend that there's no incongruity in the driving/drinking bargain that NASCAR has struck. More than 17,000 people die and a half-million are injured every year because of drunken driving.

NASCAR Defends Itself

NASCAR knows it's on dangerous ground here, no matter how lucrative the deals might be. President Mike Helton went to great pains to sugarcoat the mixed message by emphasizing the "long record of responsible advertising" by the spirits companies.

That's questionable, but there also is the real wreckage caused by drunken drivers in the 18-to-34 male demographic that NASCAR so assiduously and successfully cultivates.

"Any spirits company involved in NASCAR will have marketing campaigns strongly grounded in responsibility and will follow advertising and marketing guidelines set by NASCAR that are consistent with the Distilled Spirits Council's advertising code," Helton said.

He said NASCAR reached out to advocacy groups such as the National Commission Against Drunk Driving and Mothers Against Drunk Driving.

John Moulden, president of the National Commission Against Drunk Driving, was impressed with the way NASCAR approached the change of policy.

"They told us that any advertising done in NASCAR by breweries or distillers, they'll make sure it is directed at the legal age audience and not to kids and that they will require 20 percent of advertising dollars go toward promoting responsible drinking.

> *"Let's not cry out for a return to Prohibition but let's not kid ourselves that a sport like NASCAR, and the sponsorships behind it, doesn't influence its fans, young and old."*

"We'd like to see that same type of responsibility by all sports and advertisers."

Problem is, there are plenty of NASCAR fans under 21 watching those alcohol ads going around the track and making the obvious connection with life in the fast lane.

NASCAR's Potential to Cause Change

Wendy Hamilton, president of MADD, is holding back judgment, saying the only contact she had with NASCAR was a few e-mails and an agreement to participate on an advisory committee.

Personally, she said, she's always thought it was "absurd" to put alcohol ads on cars. But she emphasized that MADD is not a prohibitionist organization and does not oppose alcohol advertising aimed at drinkers over 21.

"NASCAR, with its fan base, has the opportunity to be a player in this world when it comes to drunk driving because clearly not enough people are getting the message," Hamilton said.

"Our position is very clear. We're going to be talking about all alcohol, not just the distilled spirits industry, and our message is no underage drinking and don't mix drinking and driving."

Every sport should be sending the same message. Binge drinking on college campuses, especially at football and basketball games, is huge.

"There isn't a single area of sports in this country where

some athlete hasn't been convicted for drunk driving or has hurt somebody driving drunk," Hamilton said.

[In early November 2004,] 19-year-old, six-time Olympic champion swimmer Michael Phelps was arrested and charged with drunken driving in Maryland, where the legal drinking age is 21.

"I want to say that last week I made a mistake. I wanted to share my feelings and I know that getting in a car with anything to drink is wrong, dangerous and is unacceptable," Phelps told The Associated Press.

Hamilton called Phelps' actions "very disappointing" but said "he still has an opportunity to be a great role model by doing the right thing and accepting the consequences and never doing it again."

NASCAR has a chance, too, to be a model for sports and do more than simply make money off its beer and liquor deals. That's a sobering thought it can't afford to pass up.

6

Alcohol Advertisements on Race Cars Do Not Promote Underage Drinking

Doug Bandow

Doug Bandow is a senior fellow with the Cato Institute, a nonprofit public policy research foundation. Bandow also writes a weekly column for newspapers across the country. He has appeared on many national television and radio shows, including Crossfire *and* Oprah.

NASCAR's recent decision to allow liquor companies to buy ad space on its racing cars has provoked the fury of critics. Those opposed to alcohol advertising on cars argue that it sends the message to underage NASCAR fans that drinking is glamorous. Some critics even believe that such ads promote drunk driving. However, studies have shown that there is no evidence that advertising leads people to increase their consumption of alcohol. Teenagers who drink state that it is peer pressure and parents, not advertising, that influence their behavior. Furthermore, the vast majority of people who attend NASCAR races or watch them on television are older than twenty-one. NASCAR also ensures that 20 percent of its ads contain messages about "responsible drinking."

NASCAR racing has long sported a blue-collar reputation. But the organization's [2004] decision to accept liquor advertising has energized the usual national nannies.

Beer marketing is everywhere. Yet few complaints are heard.

Try to sell spirits like any other legal product, however, and expect to be attacked.

When Seagrams [liquor company] abandoned its voluntary ban on broadcast ads several years ago one would have thought that cocaine merchants had seized the airwaves. Federal commissions launched investigations, Congressmen introduced legislation, commentators fulminated, and activists raged. The political furor eventually died down and cable television has since run millions of dollars worth of ads for spirits. NBC began allowing liquor ads two years ago but abandoned the practice after some congressmen threatened to hold hearings.

Now the hysterics are at it again.

The National Association for Stock Car Auto Racing recently announced it would allow spirits producers to sponsor NASCAR teams. Diageo [a multinational alcoholic beverage and food corporation] was first out of the block, with a deal to back Roush Racing with the Crown Royal brand.

NASCAR's Long Tradition of Alcohol Advertising

NASCAR's move shouldn't surprise. Liquor producers already sponsor teams in the Indy Racing League and the International Race of Champions. NASCAR allows spirits advertising at racetracks, as well as team sponsorship by malt beverages (Diageo advertises Smirnoff ICE in this way). Moreover, NASCAR has accepted beer advertising for a quarter century.

In fact, the series grew out of the practice of moonshiners outrunning "revenuers" during Prohibition. Yet today's self-anointed defenders of public virtue think the races should serve as a civic role model.

> *"An estimated 95 percent and 88 percent of race attendees and TV viewers, respectively, are over 21."*

For instance, says American Medical Association president-elect J. Edward Hill: The series "should use its new-found marketing and cultural influence to be a positive role model, not to endanger the lives and health of youth through the glamorization of liquor."

George Hacker of the so-called Center for Science in the Public Interest—a paternalistic group long worried that someone somewhere might actually enjoy eating or drinking—warned: "You'll have liquor billboards rolling around the track hundreds of times, constantly in view of the cameras."

Yet these complaints could be made against all alcohol ads.

Alcohol Advertising Does Not Promote Underage Drinking

So the critics point to kids. AP [Associated Press] sports columnist Steve Wilstein charged: "There are plenty of NASCAR fans under 21 watching those alcohol ads going around the track and making the obvious connection with life in the fast lane."

Actually, the average NASCAR fan is 38-years-old. An estimated 95 percent and 88 percent of race attendees and TV viewers, respectively, are over 21.

Some critics bizarrely link NASCAR ads to drunk driving. Charged Hacker: "Rather than disassociating drinking and driving, it reinforces the relationship between liquor and cars."

Wilstein noted that "More than 17,000 people die and a half-million are injured every year because of drunken driving."

> *"When kids explain why they drink, they cite their parents and peers, not ads."*

What does this have to do with NASCAR? Spirits producers, like beer makers, are advertising a product, not a practice: none of them gain from drunk driving. In fact, the NASCAR agreement specifies that 20 percent of race-themed ads must contain "responsible drinking" messages. John Moulden, president of the National Commission Against Drunk Driving, observed "They appear to be trying to do it right."

He added: "We'd like to see that same type of responsibility by all sports and advertisers." Although the National Highway Traffic Safety Administration has taken no position on the issue, some officials privately echo Moulden's view.

Is the problem alcohol ads in general? They are meant to

sell product, of course. But drinking alcohol is not the same as drinking irresponsibly.

Most alcohol consumed around the world isn't advertised. Studies of changes in advertising in America and overseas have found no measurable impact on total consumption. When kids explain why they drink, they cite their parents and peers, not ads.

More than a decade ago the Federal Trade Commission [FTC] admitted that there was "no reliable basis to conclude that alcohol advertising significantly affects consumption, let alone abuse."

Advertising mostly changes brand preference.

Alcohol Companies Police Themselves

The industry also regulates itself. Companies want to make money to be sure, but encouraging their best customers to die in car wrecks would be bad for business. Indeed, all of the industry associations have voluntary advertising codes covering ad content and placement.

The FTC reports: "for the most part, members of the industry comply with the current standards." Adds the Commission, "many individual companies follow their own internal standards that exceed code requirements."

Does the world still suffer from alcoholics and drunk drivers and other alcohol abusers? Sure.

Almost any good thing in life can be abused. So it is with alcohol.

But the answer is to punish those who act irresponsibly, not the product. A free society cannot allow well-intended busybodies to treat everyone else like children.

7

Tobacco Advertising Targets Youths

Campaign for Tobacco-Free Kids

The Campaign for Tobacco-Free Kids is a nonprofit organization that seeks to protect children from tobacco addiction and secondhand smoke.

The tobacco industry has found a new way to entice children and young adults to smoke: candy-flavored cigarettes. The R.J. Reynolds company has introduced Camel "Winter Blends," whose flavors include "Warm Winter Toffee" and "Winter MochaMint." The company is advertising these cigarettes in magazines with a large youth readership such as *Rolling Stone, Glamour*, and *Elle*. The ads depict a pretty young woman enjoying winter sports with a cigarette. Clearly, the company is trying to appeal to new young smokers. The "Winter Blends" product and marketing campaign is only the latest attempt by R.J. Reynolds to hook young smokers. It has also marketed the coconut-and-pineapple-flavored Kauai Kolada cigarette and the citrus-flavored Twista Lime. Furthermore, R.J. Reynolds is not the only tobacco company marketing to young people. The tobacco industry spends about $34 million per day to market cigarettes, and most of this marketing is targeted at kids. To stop this kind of unethical advertising, Congress should pass legislation that would give the U.S. Food and Drug Administration the authority to regulate tobacco products and marketing, and to ban candy-flavored cigarettes.

Campaign for Tobacco-Free Kids, "Cuddle up with Cancer: RJR's Candy Flavored 'Winter Blend' Cigarettes Show Big Tobacco Hasn't Changed," www.tobaccofreekids.org, November 16, 2004.

In the latest versions of its candy-flavored cigarettes, R.J. Reynolds has introduced Camel "Winter Blends" with flavors including "Warm Winter Toffee" and "Winter MochaMint." Ads for these cigarettes are appearing now in magazines with significant youth readership such as *Rolling Stone, Glamour, Cosmopolitan* and *Elle*. The ads feature an attractive young woman in bright green holiday garb and ice skates, cigarette in hand. RJR's online ads urge visitors to "Celebrate the wonder of Camel's Winter Blends. Whether you're skiing down the slopes or cuddling in a cabin." In fact, it would be more accurate to describe these candy-flavored cigarettes as an invitation to "cuddle up with cancer." It is outrageous that RJR would warp the holiday spirit, which celebrates life, to tempt children with a product that addicts and kills.

"It is outrageous that RJR would warp the holiday spirit, which celebrates life, to tempt children with a product that addicts and kills."

RJR's latest candy-flavored cigarettes follow the marketing this summer [2004] of other candy-flavored Camels, including the coconut and pineapple-flavored Kauai Kolada and the citrus-flavored Twista Lime. Hawai'i Governor Linda Lingle expressed outrage and stated, "Using the name of Kauai and Hawai'i images to market cigarettes to young people is disgusting." These candy-flavored cigarettes clearly have their greatest appeal to new smokers, 90 percent of whom are teens or younger. Established smokers are unlikely to give up their favorite brands for these new cigarettes, but kids will be tempted to give them a try and many will get hooked. These flavored cigarettes would fit right in on store shelves alongside mint or toffee-flavored ice cream and candy bars.

The Government Must Crack Down on Tobacco Marketing to Kids

RJR's candy-flavored cigarettes are the latest evidence that the tobacco companies are just blowing smoke when they say they have made "profound and permanent" changes in how they do business and don't market to kids, as they did recently in their opening arguments in the federal government's lawsuit against the tobacco companies. RJR's actions underscore why the U.S. Department of Justice should aggressively pursue the federal lawsuit, which seeks to stop tobacco marketing to kids and bring about other fundamental changes in industry practices.

> *"Tobacco companies have not changed and continue to market in ways that appeal to kids."*

These actions also show why Congress should pass legislation granting the U.S. Food and Drug Administration (FDA) authority to regulate tobacco products, including the authority to ban candy-flavored cigarettes and crack down on other tobacco marketing to kids. RJR played a key role in defeating the FDA legislation precisely so it could continue to engage in irresponsible marketing such as the candy-flavored cigarettes. It's no surprise that this is the same company that conducted the infamous "Joe Camel" campaign that used a cartoon character to get millions of kids to start smoking. The tobacco companies clearly will not change their harmful practices unless they are forced to do so.

Tobacco Companies Have Not Changed

RJR's candy-flavored cigarettes are the latest evidence that the tobacco companies have not changed and continue to market in ways that appeal to kids. The Federal Trade Commission [FTC] reported in October [2004] that the tobacco companies in 2002 spent a record $12.5 billion—$34.2 million a day—to market cigarettes. This represents an 85 percent increase since the November 1998 state tobacco settlement, contradicting the tobacco companies' claim that the settlement significantly restricted their marketing. The FTC report showed that almost two-thirds of cigarette marketing was spent on price discounts, which have the greatest impact on kids, who are the most price-sensitive customers. Tobacco marketing is highly effective at influencing kids. Eighty-two percent of youth smokers (ages 12–17) prefer the three most heavily advertised brands—Philip Morris' Marlboro, Lorillard's Newport and RJR's Camel—compared to less than half of smokers over 25.

While spending record amounts to market cigarettes, the tobacco companies continue to fight proven measures to reduce smoking, such as tobacco tax increases and smoke-free workplace policies. Philip Morris and RJR just spent at least $1.5 million in an unsuccessful effort to defeat an Oklahoma ballot initiative to increase the cigarette tax.

The tobacco companies talk a good game. But RJR's new candy-flavored cigarettes and the industry's other recent actions show that the tobacco companies have not changed and continue to put their own profits ahead of the nation's health.

8

Tobacco Advertising Does Not Influence Youths

Cato Institute

The Cato Institute is a nonprofit libertarian public policy research institute based in Washington, D.C.

The U.S. Senate is debating whether the Food and Drug Administration (FDA) should be responsible for monitoring and regulating advertising of cigarettes as it is for drug ads. People who support legislation for FDA regulation argue that it will help eliminate ads that target young people. However, there is no proof that tobacco advertising causes an increase in youth smoking. Rather than attracting new consumers, ads simply encourage current consumers to switch brands. Increased control over advertising by the FDA will also prevent the advertising of healthier tobacco products. In order to reduce smoking among children, state governments need to enforce penalties for underage tobacco purchase and use. In addition, parents need to exercise more responsibility to keep minors from smoking.

Under legislation introduced in June 2002 by Sens. Edward Kennedy (D-Mass.), Mike DeWine (R-Ohio), and Richard Durbin (D-Ill.), the Food and Drug Administration (FDA) would be authorized to regulate cigarette ads and ingredients, including nicotine—or to ban nicotine altogether. Lamentably, Philip Morris—the industry leader with the most to gain from restrictions

Cato Institute, *Cato Handbook for Congress, 108th*, edited by Edward H. Crane and David Boaz, www.cato.org, January 2003.

on would-be competitors—quickly chimed in to support many of the proposals. Yet, if tobacco is to be regulated as a drug, Congress will simply be guaranteeing a pervasive black market in tobacco products. FDA regulation that makes cigarettes taste like tree bark, coupled with higher prices, will inevitably foment illegal dealings dominated by criminal gangs hooking underage smokers on an adulterated product freed of all the constraints on quality that competitive markets usually afford.

> *"The real question is whether tobacco advertising can be linked to increases in aggregate consumption. There's no evidence for that link."*

The war on cigarettes, like other crusades, may have been well-intentioned at the beginning; but as zealotry takes hold, the regulations become foolish and ultimately destructive. Consider the current attempt to control tobacco advertising. Not only are the public policy implications harmful, but there are obvious First Amendment violations that should concern every American who values free expression. Our Constitution protects Klan speech, flag burning, and gangsta rap, which, by the way, directly targets teenagers. But if [golf pro] Tiger Woods showed up in an ad for Camel cigarettes, the anti-tobacco crowd would bring the boot of government down hard on the neck of R.J. Reynolds.

Advertising Does Not Attract New Smokers

Industry critics point to the impact of tobacco ads on uninformed and innocent teenagers. But the debate is not about whether teens smoke; they do. It's not about whether smoking is bad for them; it is. The real question is whether tobacco advertising can be linked to increases in aggregate consumption. There's no evidence for that link. The primary purpose of cigarette ads, like automobile ads, is to persuade consumers to switch from one manufacturer to another. Six European countries that banned all tobacco ads have seen overall sales *increase*—probably because health risks are no longer documented in the banned ads.

In 1983, the Supreme Court held that government may not

"reduce the adult population . . . to reading only what is fit for children." Thirteen years later, the Court affirmed that even vice products like alcoholic beverages are entitled to commercial speech protection. Most recently, the Court threw out Massachusetts regulations banning selected cigar and smokeless tobacco ads. Those ads are not the problem. Kids smoke because of peer pressure, because their parents smoke, and because they are rebelling against authority.

> *"Kids smoke because of peer pressure, because their parents smoke, and because they are rebelling against authority."*

If advertising were deregulated, newer and smaller tobacco companies would vigorously seek to carve out a bigger market share by emphasizing health claims that might bolster brand preference. In 1950, however, the Federal Trade Commission (FTC) foreclosed health claims—such as "less smoker's cough" —as well as tar and nicotine comparisons for *existing* brands. To get around that prohibition, aggressive companies created *new* brands, which they supported with an avalanche of health claims. Filter cigarettes grew from roughly 1 percent to 10 percent of domestic sales within four years.

Ads Can Benefit Smokers' Health

Then in 1954, the FTC tightened its restrictions by requiring scientific proof of health claims, even for new brands. The industry returned to promoting taste and pleasure; aggregate sales expanded. By 1957, scientists had confirmed the benefit of low-tar cigarettes. A new campaign of "Tar Derby" ads quickly emerged, and tar and nicotine levels collapsed 40 percent in two years. To shut down the flow of health claims, the FTC next demanded that they be accompanied by epidemiological evidence, of which none existed. The commission then negotiated a "voluntary" ban on tar and nicotine comparisons.

Not surprisingly, the steep decline in tar and nicotine ended in 1959. Seven years later, apparently alerted to the bad news, the FTC reauthorized tar and nicotine data but continued to proscribe associated health claims. Finally, in 1970 Congress banned all radio and television ads. Overall consumption has declined slowly since that time. In today's climate, the potential gains from health-related ads are undoubtedly greater than ever—for both aggressive companies and health-conscious consumers. If, however, government regulation expands, those gains will not be realized. Instead of "healthy" competition for market share, we will be treated to more imagery and personal endorsements—the very ads that anti-tobacco partisans decry.

State Governments and Parents Should Crack Down

If the imperative is to reduce smoking among children, the remedy lies with state governments, not the U.S. Congress. The sale of tobacco products to youngsters is illegal in every state. Those laws need to be vigorously enforced. Retailers who violate the law must be prosecuted. Proof of age requirements are appropriate if administered objectively and reasonably. Vending machine sales should be prohibited in areas such as arcades and schools where children are the main clientele. And if a minor is caught smoking or attempting to acquire cigarettes, his parents should be notified. Parenting is, after all, primarily the responsibility of fathers and mothers, not the government.

Instead, government has expanded its war on tobacco far beyond any legitimate concern with children's health. Mired in regulations, laws, taxes, and litigation, we look to Congress to extricate us from the mess it helped create. Yet if Congress authorizes the FDA to regulate cigarette ads and control the content of tobacco products, it will exacerbate the problem. Equally important, Congress will have delegated excessive and ill-advised legislative authority to an unelected administrative agency, and set the stage for significant intrusions on commercial free speech.

9
Smokeless-Tobacco Advertising Increases Teen Tobacco Use

Matthew Myers

Matthew Myers is president and CEO of the Campaign for Tobacco-Free Kids, which seeks to reduce tobacco use among children. It also aims to counter the influence of the tobacco industry and its special interests. The following remarks are excerpted from Myers's statement to the U.S. House Energy and Commerce Committee about the dangers of smokeless tobacco and its advertising.

Smokeless tobacco products include chewing tobacco, lozenges, and gum—all of which contain nicotine. Although tobacco companies advertise these products as being less harmful than cigarettes, smokeless tobacco poses comparable health risks. In addition, the companies are targeting children by adding candy flavoring to their smokeless tobacco products, which clearly appeals to young people. Since the Master Settlement Agreement of 1998, in which tobacco companies were prohibited from targeting minors in their advertising, smokeless-tobacco advertising expenditures have actually increased. Many of the tobacco companies' claims that smokeless products are less harmful than cigarettes are based on data from smokeless-tobacco use in Sweden. However, this comparison is invalid because Swedish smokeless tobacco contains fewer harmful chemicals than its American counterpart. Finally, claims that smokeless tobacco products pose fewer health risks than cigarettes may

Matthew Myers, statement before the U.S. House Energy and Commerce Subcommittee, Washington, DC, June 3, 2003.

cause smokers simply to switch tobacco products when they would otherwise have given up tobacco altogether.

Let us start with a basic premise: smokeless tobacco products as sold in the United States have been found to increase the risk of oral cancer and other serious diseases. The Surgeon General, the National Cancer Institute, the American Cancer Society, the American Dental Association, the Scientific Advisory Committee to the World Health Organization and numerous other scientific bodies have all determined that there is conclusive evidence that smokeless tobacco products as sold in the United States increase the risk of serious disease. This conclusion is no surprise. Scientists have identified twenty-eight cancer-causing chemicals in these products.

Smokeless Claims to Be Safer

Today we are seeing history repeat itself. Just as we had the last time this committee met to discuss smokeless tobacco [in the 1980s], we have a smokeless tobacco industry that refuses to acknowledge the health effects of its products seeking government approval to use health-related claims in advertising, whether or not that advertising's primary appeal is to children. In 1985 the then President of the Smokeless Tobacco Council testified before this committee "it has not been scientifically established smokeless tobacco is a cause of any human disease." In April 1999, a spokesperson for the United States Smokeless Tobacco Company, a subsidiary of U.S. Tobacco (UST) was quoted in the *Providence Journal* as claiming that it has not been "scientifically established" that smokeless tobacco is "a cause of oral cancer." This statement resulted in the Rhode Island Attorney General suing UST for violating the multi-state settlement agreement's prohibition on making false statements about the health effects of its tobacco products. UST was required to pay $15,000 to the Attorney General's office to fund efforts to prevent youth tobacco use and to formally acknowledge that the Surgeon General and other public health authorities have concluded that smokeless tobacco is addictive and can cause oral cancer.

[In 2002], UST claimed in a letter to the Federal Trade Commission (FTC) that "smokeless tobacco has not been shown to be a cause of any human disease." UST would have this committee think that it is new evidence that has motivated it to seek approval to market its products as a safer alternative to cigarettes. The unfortunate reality is that this is a company that has never acknowledged that its products cause harm. How can you have a meaningful discussion about the potential to use a cancer-causing product to reduce the harm from smoking with an industry that won't acknowledge that its products cause harm and hasn't agreed to meaningful government regulation?

Smokeless Advertising Promotes Youth Tobacco Use

There is a second basic point about which there can be no dispute. [In the 1970s] few young people in this country used smokeless tobacco products. However, in large part in response to a massive marketing campaign that in part portrayed smokeless tobacco use as safer than cigarette smoking, the number of people who used these products and the demographics of who used these products changed in the early 1980's. Smokeless tobacco usage among young males rose dramatically. As a nation we experienced a sixty percent upswing in smokeless tobacco use among young men resulting from a decade of smokeless advertising. The lesson is clear: in the absence of meaningful government regulation, our children are vulnerable to smokeless tobacco marketing that portrays smokeless tobacco use in a manner that kids find acceptable. Largely because the major smokeless tobacco manufacturers have fought FDA regulation of both their products and their marketing, our kids are as vulnerable today as they were 25 years ago.

Was it an accident that smokeless tobacco use rose in the 1980's even as the leading smokeless tobacco companies argued that they didn't market to kids? The answer from their own documents is no. According to internal company documents, UST developed a graduation strategy some time ago for hooking kids as new smokeless tobacco users. As one document states:

> "New users of smokeless tobacco—attracted to the product for a variety of reasons—are most likely to begin with products that are milder tasting, more flavored, and/or easier to control in the mouth. After a period of time, there is a natural progression of product switching to brands that are more full-bodied, less flavored, have more concentrated 'tobacco taste' than the entry brand."

UST has also used the addition of flavorings to increase the appeal of its products to children. In 1993, cherry flavoring was added to UST's Skoal Long Cut, an entry or starter product. A former UST sales representative revealed that, "Cherry Skoal is for somebody who likes the taste of candy, if you know what I'm saying."

Master Settlement Fails to Change Marketing Practices

Many had hoped that when the United States Smokeless Tobacco Company signed [the Master Settlement Agreement (MSA)] with the states in 1998, its marketing practices would change dramatically. It did not happen because UST has apparently interpreted the broad prohibition against targeting youth as not requiring it to change the kind of advertising and youth oriented imagery that it has previously used that has made its products so appealing to children. A May 2002 study by the Massachusetts Department of Public Health found that UST's overall magazine advertising increased 135% from 1997 to 2001. The study also found that UST's advertising in magazines with high youth readership increased 161% during the same time period. For the period 1997–2001, UST's expenditures in youth magazines increased from $3.6 million to $9.4 million. Thus, smokeless tobacco advertising that appeals to children has continued unabated. One only has to look at the images projected by this advertising to understand its appeal to children. While UST may increase or decrease its advertising in certain magazines for its own purposes when it chooses, the evidence is that the MSA has not provided the legal club that was anticipated. In addition, although the multi-state settlement agreement has limited UST's ability to continue to do brand name sponsorships of some events and teams, UST continues to be a promotional sponsor of both professional motor sports and rodeo and bull riding. . . .

There is a third fundamental point—not all smokeless tobacco products are alike. UST has continued to market products far higher in one cancer-causing class of agents—nitrosamines—than its counterparts in Sweden, despite the technical ability to produce low nitrosamine products. Data concerning Swedish *snus* [snuff] is often cited by UST in support of its desire to market its products—all of its products, including its products with very high nitrosamine levels—as a way to reduce the risks of tobacco use because of some data that indicates that it has not been associated with an increase in cancer in Sweden. Swedish smokeless products are much lower in cancer-causing nitrosamines than U.S. products. . . .

Swedish *snus* is also controlled for heavy metals found in smokeless tobacco products, like cadmium, lead, nickel and chromium, as well as substances such as arsenic, BaP's [benzapyrene], and pesticides. None of those controls apply to American products. It is for these reasons that organizations like the Scientific Advisory Council to the World Health Organization in November 2002 distinguished between the evidence that it found conclusively linked U.S. smokeless tobacco products and oral cancer and the evidence that it found that the health effects of Swedish *snus* were more uncertain.

Stricter Marketing Rules in Sweden

There is a third distinction between what is described as the Swedish experience and the likely result in the U.S. The marketing and advertising of smokeless products in the United States and Sweden is completely different. Sweden forbids the marketing and advertising of all tobacco products, and no claims in advertising about relative safety of these products are permitted. In the United States there are few restrictions on the advertising and marketing of smokeless tobacco products, and UST wants to make explicit claims about the relative safety of its products.

> *"In the absence of meaningful government regulation, our children are vulnerable to smokeless tobacco marketing that portrays smokeless tobacco use in a manner that kids find acceptable."*

The difference in the laws governing marketing in the two countries is critical. When [the Campaign for Tobacco-Free Kids] met with representatives of UST and asked if they believed that there was anything to prevent UST from using ads featuring roosters with what we perceived to be youth-oriented slogans placed in youth-oriented magazines to promote their products as less hazardous than cigarettes, they were quick to say no. They went further. UST said that if they were given permission to claim that their products were less hazardous than cigarettes, it was their belief that the FTC did not have the legal authority to tell them what kinds of ads or magazines those claims could appear in.

Claims Could Dissuade Smokers from Quitting

There is a fourth fundamental point. Another potential risk to permitting smokeless tobacco to be marketed as a harm reduction mechanism in the absence of meaningful government regulation is that claims of risk reduction could lead smokers who would otherwise quit not to do so. The risk is real. In August 2001, UST announced plans to market a new smokeless tobacco product called Revel. UST is marketing the new product as a way to consume tobacco in places or situations when smoking is not allowed or is not socially acceptable. Many smokers quit after the enactment of restrictions on smoking in the workplace. There is legitimate concern that in the absence of any regulation of where and how smokeless tobacco products are marketed, some current cigarette smokers who would otherwise quit will switch instead to Revel or other smokeless products. This concern is compounded by studies that how that claims of reduced risk can lead consumers to falsely underestimate the relative benefits of quitting versus switching. . . .

Harm Reduction Ads Premature

A discussion about harm reduction has to begin with a discussion about providing the FDA with the kind of authority that is necessary to protect consumers, verify claims, and require that all reasonable steps are taken to reduce the harm caused to smokers. Is there a role for smokeless tobacco in a comprehensive effort to reduce the death toll from tobacco overseen by the FDA? No one has the information to make that decision today. The FDA should be open to all strategies that are scientifically based and that will save lives. The decision about what role smokeless tobacco plays in that overall scheme is a decision that can only be made by the FDA after it has all of the relevant information before it.

10

Smokeless-Tobacco Advertising Informs Smokers of Healthier Alternatives

John K. Carlisle

John K. Carlisle is the editor of Organization Trends *and* Foundation Watch *at the Capital Research Center, an organization that researches and analyzes the activities of nonprofit organizations.*

Research indicates that smokeless forms of tobacco carry fewer health risks than smoking. Both the University of Alabama–Birmingham and the American Council on Science and Health have presented substantial scientific evidence that smokeless tobacco is safer than cigarettes. However, antismoking organizations tend to favor a "quit-or-die" approach to tobacco use. They do not wish to inform the public of the reduced risks associated with smokeless tobacco and have fought the U.S. Smokeless Tobacco Company's efforts to do so. Two antismoking groups that have led the fight are the Campaign for Tobacco-Free Kids and Oral Health America. While these groups recognize that smokeless tobacco may be less harmful, they believe that any type of tobacco endorsement is irresponsible and that Americans deserve to be given information about smokeless tobacco so they can decide on the best course of action for themselves.

John K. Carlisle, "The Dangerous Anti-Smoking Lobby," CRC *Organization Trends*, www.capitalresearch.org, July 2003.

For four decades the anti-tobacco lobby has been on a crusade against cigarette smoking. Groups like the American Cancer Society, the American Heart Association and the American Lung Association have been waging intensive education campaigns on the hazards of smoking and they have lobbied government agencies and private employers to join them in issuing public appeals and warnings. This campaign has been largely successful. In 1965, the year the federal government first ordered health warning labels on cigarette packs, more than 42 percent of U.S. adults smoked. By 2000, the number had been cut to about 25 percent.

Health groups can take credit for helping reduce smoking rates and improving public health. But their "quit-or-die" strategy has about run its course. One-quarter of U.S. adults—46 million people—still smoke despite the well-known health risks. It is estimated that 400,000 Americans die each year from lung cancer and other smoking-related diseases. These committed smokers present a major policy challenge to public health authorities and advocacy groups.

Spreading the Word on Smokeless Tobacco

In recent years, scientists have discovered an accumulating body of evidence suggesting that not all forms of tobacco use are equally lethal. For instance, studies show that smokeless tobacco—popularly known as snuff tobacco—is safer than smoking tobacco. If attempts were made to convert smokers to smokeless tobacco use there is an increasing likelihood that major public health benefits will result. Scientific research suggests that rates of lung and oral cancer, emphysema and heart disease can be dramatically reduced.

Why don't we hear anything about this? The main reason is that the anti-tobacco lobby rejects all efforts to educate smokers about safer tobacco alternatives. In 2002, the U.S. Smokeless Tobacco Company (USSTC), a major manufacturer of smokeless tobacco, petitioned the federal government, requesting that it be allowed to advertise the *relative* health benefits of smokeless tobacco use.

The anti-tobacco lobby would have none of it. Blinded by a zealous adherence to a "quit-or-die" scare strategy, two groups that represent a new generation of anti-smoking activists spearheaded a lobbying campaign to have the Federal Trade Commission (FTC) reject the petition request.

The groups—the Campaign for Tobacco-Free Kids and Oral Health America—ignore the nearly 50 million consumers who have made a decision to disregard "quit-or-die" warnings. These tobacco consumers have a right to know the relative risks posed by different kinds of tobacco products on the market. But for the sake of their own unyielding policy preferences, Campaign for Tobacco-Free Kids and Oral Health America have chosen to endanger lives that could be saved if only smokers had access to more information. . . .

The Role of Anti-Smoking Groups

Today there are dozens of nonprofits that have enlisted in the war on tobacco. One current campaign is the battle to thwart information about the relative benefits of smokeless tobacco. In February 2002, 39 public health groups signed a letter to the FTC asking it to reject USSTC's petition to tout the less harmful effects of smokeless tobacco. The groups included the American Cancer Society, American Heart Association, American Lung Association, American Dental Association, American Academy of Family Physicians, Partnership for Prevention, Pharmacy Council on Tobacco Dependence and a number of lesser-known anti-smoking groups.

The most prestigious groups on the list are among the richest: American Heart Association has $502 million in revenues; $852 million in assets (2001); American Cancer Society—$322 million; $359 million (2000); American Lung Association—$24 million; $33 million (2001). By lending their names to the FTC petition these major organizations provide credibility to the activists' all-or-nothing fight against smokeless tobacco. However, two groups are the main enemies of smokeless tobacco.

Campaign for Tobacco-Free Kids

The Campaign for Tobacco-Free Kids was founded in 1996. It describes itself as "one of the nation's largest non-governmental initiatives ever launched to protect children from tobacco addiction and exposure to secondhand smoke." Its primary mission is to "de-glamorize" tobacco use by countering what it claims is tobacco company marketing aimed at children and by changing federal, state and local government policies. The Washington, DC-based group has 146 partner organizations, including the National Parent Teachers Association, National

Council of Churches, Girl Scouts of the U.S.A., Children's Defense Fund, Sierra Club, and the American Medical Association.

In 2001, Campaign for Tobacco-Free Kids reported $5.3 million in income. Most of that funding comes from the Robert Wood Johnson Foundation, which donated $3.6 million in 2001. . . .

Matthew Myers is president of Campaign for Tobacco-Free Kids. A veteran anti-tobacco crusader, Myers worked for the Federal Trade Commission's Division of Advertising Practices in the early 1980s. There he was responsible for the FTC's tobacco-related activity. Before joining the Campaign in 1996, initially as its executive vice president and chief legal counsel, Myers was general counsel for the Coalition on Smoking OR Health, an advocacy group created by the American Cancer Society, American Lung Association, and American Heart Association. During his long career Myers has been credited with helping to ban TV ads for cigarettes, mandate more stringent cigarette health warnings, raise the federal tobacco excise tax, and eliminate smoking on domestic airline flights.

Myers maintains he doesn't want to ban tobacco use. "No one thinks it's realistic or good social policy to legally ban the manufacture or sale of tobacco products," he says. "It will not work, and it will not accomplish public health goals." Myers also says it is important "to reduce the harm that tobacco products cause." Such comments seem to suggest that Myers would keep an open mind about encouraging smokeless tobacco use *among current smokers* to reduce smoking-related cancers and other diseases.

But Myers emphatically opposes letting companies advertise the less harmful effects of smokeless tobacco. He doesn't deny that smokeless tobacco is safer than smoking. However, like many anti-tobacco crusaders, he insists that advertisement is a slippery slope. Ads for smokeless tobacco will inevitably lead to smoking and thus negate any public health benefits.

Oral Health America

In 2000, Chicago-based Oral Health America (OHA) joined with former U.S. Surgeon General Dr. C. Everett Koop to launch a multi-year Oral Health Initiative. It follows on OHA's "National Spit Tobacco Education Program," which was launched in 1994. From 1997 to 2003 the program received $6 million in grants from the Robert Wood Johnson Foundation. It directly challenges the proponents of smokeless tobacco and works in cooperation with Major League Baseball, the Major League Baseball Players Association and prominent sportscasters to undermine the appeal of chewing tobacco among young aspiring baseball players.

In 2001, OHA reported income of $6.9 million. Like Campaign for Tobacco-Free Kids, the Robert Wood Johnson Foundation is the primary donor, contributing $5.1 million in 2001.

Like the Campaign, OHA mobilizes opposition to any smokeless tobacco advertising. OHA President Robert Klaus calls the FTC petition "ludicrous and dangerous." He says, "It is less dangerous to jump out of a 3rd floor window than a 10th floor window, but no responsible citizen and certainly no health authority, would propose either."

Smokeless Is Safer

In 1995 two University of Alabama, Birmingham (UAB) scientists published an article in *Priorities For Health,* the health journal of the American Council on Science and Health, which explained why Klaus is wrong. Their research argues that switching from cigarettes to smokeless tobacco will benefit public health.

Dr. Brad Rodu and Dr. Philip Cole noted that smoke was the most obvious difference between the two tobacco products. Smoke is why cigarettes, pipes and cigars are dangerous. Nicotine is addictive, but it is not the source of cancer and other diseases. In their article, "Would a Switch from Cigarettes to Smokeless Tobacco Benefit Public Health?—Yes," Rodu, a professor of anatomic pathology and senior scientist at the University's Comprehensive Cancer Center, and Cole, a professor of epidemiology at UAB's school of public health, noted that smokeless tobacco does not cause lung cancer, emphysema or other diseases of the lung, and it doesn't pose excessive heart attack risks. Moreover, they observed that smokeless tobacco obviously causes no second-hand smoke, which the American Heart Association claims is responsible for 40,000 U.S. deaths each year.

Anti-smoking advocates have countered that smokeless tobacco produces its own ills. For example, it leads to a higher incidence of oral cancer. A 1981 study in *The New England Journal of Medicine* concluded that smokeless tobacco users are four times more likely to develop oral cancer than nonusers. Says Dr. David Connolly, head of tobacco control programs for the Massachusetts Department of Health, "It's like trying to play

God—trading oral cancer for lung cancer."

But Rodu and Cole respond that smokers are still far more likely to develop oral cancer than smokeless users. Indeed, using smokeless tobacco instead of smoking tobacco reduces the risk of developing oral cancer by about 50 percent. Because smokeless tobacco poses no danger of lung cancer, lung disease, and heart disease, and because the threat of oral cancer is sharply reduced, Rodu and Cole estimate that it is *98 percent safer than cigarette smoking*. They note: "The number of deaths from smoking is almost 70 times higher than the number from smokeless tobacco use. In terms of life expectancy, the smokeless-tobacco user loses only about 15 days on average, compared with the eight years lost by the smoker."

"*If consumers will not voluntarily abandon tobacco products entirely, or if banning tobacco use is not feasible, then it is worthwhile to consider a next-best step: promoting* safer *alternatives that can benefit public health.*"

The dispute about whether to switch from smoking to smokeless tobacco goes to the heart of a larger public policy debate over what's known as "harm reduction" theory. "Harm reduction" is a claim that says it is sometimes impractical to eliminate health risks entirely or that trying to eliminate a health risk will produce an undesirable social side effect. In these cases, other steps should be taken to ameliorate the problem. In other words, a "harm reduction" approach to disease looks at the "next-best step." If consumers will not voluntarily abandon tobacco products entirely, or if banning tobacco use is not feasible, then it is worthwhile to consider a next-best step: promoting *safer* alternatives that can benefit public health.

The "Switch-to-Smokeless" Strategy

Instead of "quit-or-die," many supporters of a harm reduction policy approach to the hazards of smoking favor a "switch-to-smokeless" strategy. This has major implications for improving public health.

If 46 million smokers were to switch to smokeless tobacco,

Rodu and Cole estimate that the number of people who die annually from tobacco-related cancer would drop from 151,000 to 6,000. The 6,000 smokeless-related deaths would be almost exclusively due to oral cancer. But this still represents a significant decrease from the 11,500 smokers who currently die from oral cancer.

In addition, a switch to smokeless tobacco would yield even more dramatic reductions in tobacco-related diseases:

• The number of people dying from heart and circulatory disease would drop from 180,000 to 0

• Number dying from respiratory disease would drop from 85,000 to 0

• Number dying from miscellaneous causes would drop from 3,000 to 0

Thus, if 46 million U.S. smokers switched to smokeless tobacco, the number dying annually from tobacco-related diseases would drop from 419,000 to 6,000.

Dr. Rodu asks, "Do we withhold this information from those smokers who are desperate to quit and have tried all conventional approaches that require abstinence from tobacco?"

It's noteworthy that no one has challenged the legitimacy of Rodu and Cole's findings—including Matthew Myers and the Campaign for Tobacco-Free Kids.

Rodu and Cole also are receiving important institutional support from the American Council on Science and Health (ACSH). With a board of 350 doctors, scientists and policy advisors, ACSH addresses consumer health issues involving food, nutrition, chemicals, pharmaceuticals, the environment, and smoking. No one has ever accused ACSH of being a friend of the tobacco industry. Indeed, in a 1997 article in *Priorities For Health,* ACSH president Dr. Elizabeth Whelan wrote: "We will not be able truly to realign our health priorities until Congress strips the cigarette industry of its privileged legal status and levels the playing field so that the manufacturers of the leading cause of death are forced to scrimmage on the same legal and regulatory turf as the rest of corporate America."

Yet, ACSH endorses the smokeless tobacco alternative. In a February 14, 2002, article, "The Case for Chaw," Dr. Whelan reviewed the results of Rodu and Cole's study and agreed with their recommendation on "harm reduction" grounds. Smokeless tobacco is a safer alternative to a failing "quit-or-die" approach. Said Whelan, "While those of us in public health would like a tobacco-free society in our future, any improvement is welcome."

When other anti-smoking advocates criticized her position, Whelan responded: "The data contrasting mortality figures between smoking and chewing are so staggering—over 400,000 tobacco deaths from cigarettes, an estimated 6,000 if all current smokers eventually switched to smokeless—that I do not see how in good conscience we can forbid the manufacturers of smokeless brands to make that point."

Whelan's endorsement prompted false accusations that Rodu and Cole's research was funded by a tobacco company. Dr. Rodu answers, "The research to which Dr. Whelan referred . . . was developed in a series of epidemiologic research papers appearing in peer-reviewed scientific literature and supported solely by university funds.". . .

Fighting the Promotion of Smokeless Tobacco

On February 5, 2002, the U.S. Smokeless Tobacco Company (USSTC) asked the Federal Trade Commission for permission to run ads touting the public health benefits of switching from smoking to smokeless tobacco. USSTC is the leading distributor of smokeless tobacco products in the U.S. Its popular brand names include Skoal and Copenhagen. The company did not ask that the current warning label on its products be diminished. However, it did want to add language publicizing the less harmful effects of smokeless tobacco compared to cigarette smoking. In its petition letter, the company recommended the following or similar language:

> "The Surgeon General in 1986 concluded that smokeless tobacco 'is not a safe substitute for smoking cigarettes.' While not asserting that smokeless tobacco is 'safe,' many researchers in the public health community have expressed the opinion that the use of smokeless tobacco involves significantly less risk of adverse health effects than smoking cigarettes. For those smokers who do not quit, a growing number of researchers advocate switching to smokeless tobacco products."

The Campaign for Tobacco-Free Kids immediately opposed the petition. In a February 6 [2002] statement, Myers said, "In the guise of claiming it wants to reduce the harm caused by tobacco use, UST Inc. has embarked on a strategy that risks achieving the opposite result by addicting a new generation of smokeless tobacco users." Myers never disputed that smokeless tobacco is less harmful than cigarette smoking. Furthermore, he claimed to favor truthful tobacco advertising and marketing safer tobacco products: "The debate is not about whether tobacco companies should be encouraged to reduce the harm caused by their products. They should be." But Myers still charged that USSTC was undermining efforts to warn the public about the health risks of tobacco use.

Myers then organized a coalition of all the major anti-smoking groups. In a February 25 [2002] coalition letter to the FTC, Myers claimed the petition amounted to a request that the agency "overturn the scientific conclusions of the U.S. Surgeon General, the National Cancer Institute and every other major scientific and public health agency that has examined the health effects of smokeless tobacco." The charge was wildly inaccurate. USSTC proposed no change in the existing warning label: "Smokeless tobacco is not a safe substitute for smoking cigarettes." It only proposed adding a scientifically accurate statement: Smokeless tobacco "involves significantly less risk of adverse health effects than smoking."

"Smokeless tobacco use, although definitely not without disease risks of its own, is unarguably less risky than smoking."

The battle lines were drawn. Myers' coalition consisted of 39 public health groups, including the American Heart Association, American Lung Association, American Cancer Society, American Dental Association, and Oral Health America. They would hammer home the claim that smokeless tobacco was a "gateway drug" luring more people into tobacco use, including cigarette smoking. During the ensuing months of debate, Myers repeatedly alleged: "[U.S. Smokeless Tobacco Co.] claims that it only wishes to promote its products as a 'safer' alternative . . . The result would not be few smokers, but more smokeless tobacco users and more addiction, disease and death." The coalition's "gateway" assertion gave politicians cover. In June [2002], Rep. Henry Waxman (D-CA) and Senator Richard Durbin (D-IL) wrote the FTC asking that it deny the USSTC request.

Oral Health America launched a companion media campaign. OHA president Robert Klaus hosted a July press conference featuring Connecticut Attorney General Richard Blumenthal, baseball celebrity Joe Garagiola, and Guren Von Behrens, an oral cancer survivor. Garagiola, the chairman of OHA's National Spit Tobacco Education Program, described how he chewed tobacco for years but stopped after his daughter wondered if he would die. Behrens, his face severely disfigured, made an especially compelling appeal. OHA later asked Dr. Richard Carmona, the new U.S. Surgeon General, to condemn USSTC's petition.

USSTC withdrew the petition in August 2002. It argued for a delay in government action in view of new research coming from Europe that would shed more light on how smokeless tobacco was helping reduce tobacco-related cancer and other diseases. But Myers declared victory: *"The USSTC petition was a bad idea from the beginning and should not be resurrected. This petition was always about increasing the numbers of people who use smokeless tobacco rather than reducing the harm caused by tobacco."*

Myers and Klaus show no sign that they will abandon the failing "quit-or-die" anti-smoking strategy that grows ever more shrill as its effectiveness dims. Unfortunately, U.S. Surgeon General Carmona is in agreement with the anti-tobacco lobby. At a June 3, 2003, congressional hearing, he erroneously stated that "there is no significant scientific evidence that suggests smokeless tobacco is a safer alternative to cigarettes."

But smoking opponents like David Sweanor, a lawyer with the Toronto-based Nonsmokers Rights' Association, say the public would benefit from advertising about the less adverse health effects of smokeless tobacco. "There is a huge difference in disease risk between combustion and noncombustion forms of tobacco," says Sweanor.

U.S. public health spokesmen are beginning to break down the wall of silence on the smokeless tobacco option. Echoing European experts, academics like Kenneth C. Warner of the University of Michigan School of Public Health say, "Smokeless tobacco use, although definitely not without disease risks of its own, is unarguably less risky than smoking."

To the uncompromising zealots at Campaign for Tobacco-Free Kids and the rest of the anti-smoking lobby, there can be no alternative that satisfies their purist principles. But don't nearly 50 million Americans deserve information that could save their lives? Don't they deserve a chance to make up their own minds?

11

Hollywood Must Stop Glamorizing Smoking in Movies

Stanton Glantz

Stanton Glantz is a professor of medicine at the University of California–San Francisco (UCSF) and director of the UCSF Center for Tobacco Control Research and Education. His publications include The Cigarette Papers *and* Tobacco War.

Tobacco and Hollywood have been longtime partners in advertising. For many years, movie producers accepted payments or other incentives to depict smoking in movies. By glorifying smoking, this practice arguably encouraged young people to smoke. Since the tobacco industry agreed to stop colluding with movie producers, smoking portrayals have only increased. The producers and tobacco companies are both to blame. There are four simple measures that could alleviate this problem: state in the movie credits that no one involved in the production received an incentive to display tobacco, require that antitobacco ads run before the films, cease identifying particular brands in movies, and give movies showing smoking an R rating.

Fighting secondhand smoke for nearly 25 years, I've learned the enemy isn't the poor smoker. It's the tobacco industry. Big Tobacco knows its future riches depend, more than anything else, on social acceptance. Without it, ashtrays will go the way of the spittoon. But acceptance must be constantly manu-

Stanton Glantz, "Commentary: What to Do About Hollywood: Tobacco's Smoldering Affair; Despite Measure Taken Years Ago, On-Screen Smoking Is on the Rise. But There Are Ways to Control the Damage," *Los Angeles Times*, June 2, 2001.

factured. And Hollywood has always been in on the act. . . .

In contrast to the health groups, who saw smoking as a medical issue, the tobacco industry has always seen smoking as a cultural issue.

> *"For 80 years the tobacco industry has addicted hundreds of millions of men and women with the help of Hollywood movies."*

And there is no better way to control pop culture worldwide than through movies. Tobacco mass marketing and Hollywood pop culture grew up together, businesslike twins joined at the hip. For 80 years the tobacco industry has addicted hundreds of millions of men and women with the help of Hollywood movies—and, later, TV—that portrayed smoking as glamorous, sexy, adult. Stars once explicitly endorsed tobacco brands in magazine ads and TV commercials. Now they implicitly endorse brands by using them in the movies. There's actually been an upswing in movie smoking over the last few years. Is it corruption? Or stupidity?

It's the rich, powerful and glamorous who smoke in the movies, when in reality it's the depressed, poor and less educated who smoke. It doesn't matter if the good guys or the bad guys smoke. Large studies have shown that the more smoking in the movies kids see, the more likely they are to start smoking.

Tobacco Endorsed in Movies

Hollywood and Big Tobacco's incestuous affair puts the film "Chinatown" to shame. The secret history, uncovered in tons of corporate files produced by recent lawsuits, shows the two industries colluded to get around the 1970 TV ban on tobacco advertising. L.A.'s biggest PR firms brokered endorsements with some of the film industry's biggest names. Publicity was bought for as little as free cartons. This hasn't stopped. *Vanity Fair*'s Oscar party this year [2001] featured bowls of free cigarettes, whose generous donors hope paparazzi will snap the smoking stars.

The handshake deal was to keep big stars publicly smoking, place tobacco brands on the scene and include tobacco advertising in the frame. Just as important, the tobacco industry pushed negative images out. Onscreen smoking was supposed to project fantasies of sexuality and power, good or bad, always dramatic—never the ugly, banal realities of addiction, disease and death.

As you might expect, the seduction was mutual. Here's how one producer shrewdly, accurately pitched RJ Reynolds: "Film is better than any commercial that has been run on television or in any magazine because the audience is totally unaware of any sponsor involvement."

By the late 1980s, things got so giddy that one star agreed to take $500,000 from Brown & Williamson Tobacco to show its brands in his next five movies. Meanwhile, rival Philip Morris agreed to pay $350,000 to have James Bond smoke Larks. Even Superman was implicated—Lois Lane chain-smoked Marlboros and Superman II saved the world by bursting from a giant Marlboro logo.

Smoking Ban Has Opposite Effect

Shaken by congressional hearings on such shenanigans in 1989, Big Tobacco promised to stop paying for smoking in the movies. They promised again in 1998 when they settled tobacco litigation brought by the states. But the plot has only thickened since then. There is actually more smoking in the movies now than 10 years ago, before the tobacco industry's voluntary ban on smoking in the movies. And the brands most heavily advertised in other media are the ones most likely to show up on the big screen. Hollywood covets the 18-to-24-year-old demographic, and so does Big Tobacco. Coincidence? Marlboro scores the most screen appearances in Hollywood movies; it also owns the market of young, new smokers.

U.S. teens aren't the only victims. Hollywood movies offer a major marketing vehicle for Big Tobacco overseas. Outside the American media spotlight, celebrities such as Antonio Banderas and Charlie Sheen have shilled for Parliament (Philip Morris, yet again) in TV spots and print ads from Japan to Argentina. How can we possibly believe that Hollywood has sworn off Big Tobacco?

Sharing the Responsibility

Tobacco companies are longtime liars and deniers, so we can hardly turn to them for candor. As late as 1994, their executives swore under oath that nicotine wasn't addictive. They certainly didn't come fully clean about their Hollywood connections in 1989. But what about the Hollywood community? Why is it serving a racket that's buried many of its most gifted members and continues to kill 3 million people each year?

> *"By the late 1980s, things got so giddy that one star agreed to take $500,000 from Brown & Williamson Tobacco to show its brands in his next five movies."*

Perhaps we should pity A-list stars who confuse their own addictions with valid artistic choices—and insist on smoking while cameras roll. Maybe we should cock a cliched eyebrow at directors and writers who lazily rely on what Stella Adler called "cigarette acting" to build character. Or maybe we should ask if Hollywood studios—many of them now part of huge media conglomerates—are quietly stroking the tobacco industry for advertising heavily in magazines belonging to the same corporate litter. Payola, after all, is effective only if it can't be seen.

Because of concern over the growing pro-tobacco influence of movies, I have spent the last 10 years quietly attending meetings and conferences with people from the entertainment industry trying to "raise consciousness" about this problem. As a professor, I also value creativity and intellectual freedom and hoped to make progress through quiet discussion. While I met many good people, the power structure in the movie industry simply repeated the same sort of hackneyed arguments about the 1st Amendment that we hear so often from their friends in the tobacco industry. This isn't about the 1st Amendment or freedom of expression, and the solution isn't censorship, a cure as bad as the disease.

Simple and Effective Solutions

We know people were crassly paid off in the past. We know there's more smoking in movies now than before. We also know that smoking doesn't sell movie tickets. It sells cigarettes to kids who watch PG-13- and R-rated movies and videos. Knowing all that—and knowing Big Tobacco so well—I propose four modest but effective fixes:

• Certify in the end credits that nobody on the production received anything of value—cash, loans, smokes, publicity, nada—in exchange for using or displaying tobacco.

• Require genuinely strong anti-tobacco advertisements—not produced by the tobacco industry or its fronts—to run before films with any tobacco presence. This will help immunize audiences without intruding on the film's content.

• Stop identifying brands. For leads like Nicolas Cage, Angelina Jolie, Brad Pitt or Julia Roberts to smoke a Marlboro or any other brand on screen is worth far, far more to Big Tobacco than a traditional advertisement.

• Rate any film with smoking an R. Kids who start smoking say they expect to quit within five years. They don't. One-third will eventually die from tobacco—far more than from gun violence, let alone foul language in a film.

None of these four measures requires government action. None will choke creativity or restrict content. Each will make American movies much less complicit in the global tobacco epidemic.

Now what's the excuse?

12

Tobacco Companies Are Working to Stop Depictions of Smoking in Movies

Vanessa O'Connell

Vanessa O'Connell is a staff reporter at the Wall Street Journal, *a daily publication of Dow Jones & Company that monitors financial and business news.*

According to the 1998 Master Settlement Agreement between tobacco companies and the California state attorneys general, movie producers may not accept money or other incentives to portray smoking in their films. Despite this restriction, movies continue to depict smoking and show specific tobacco products such as Marlboro and Camel cigarettes. Under pressure to reduce the appeal of cigarettes to young people, tobacco companies are trying to stop these depictions but are meeting many obstacles. Film producers argue that they have a First Amendment right to show tobacco products in their movies and that the portrayals are part of their artistic vision. However, tobacco companies continue to fight to prevent their products from being used in movies.

In Paramount Pictures' recent film "Twisted," Samuel L. Jackson portrays a police commissioner who, at one dramatic moment, lights up a Marlboro cigarette.

Marlboro maker Philip Morris USA didn't request the plug,

but it would seem to be a welcome publicity windfall, particularly now that cigarettes can no longer be advertised on billboards, television or through product placements.

Instead, Philip Morris owner Altria Group Inc. is asking the studio behind "Twisted" to go back to the editing room—to take the Marlboros out.

Tobacco Companies Want Cigarette-Free Films

"We believe the motion-picture industry should voluntarily refrain from portraying or referring to cigarette brands or brand imagery in movies," wrote Philip Morris Senior Vice President Howard Willard III in a May 20, [2004,] letter to Viacom Inc.'s Paramount. Philip Morris asked the studio to remove Marlboros from all versions of "Twisted" licensed for future broadcast, including the forthcoming DVD, set for release Aug. 31, [2004].

Facing unprecedented pressure to reduce the allure of cigarettes to youth, major cigarette marketers are making an unexpected new plea to Hollywood: remove references to cigarette brands from films and scripts.

The push comes as state authorities in California have begun to inform tobacco companies that they are obliged to police the use of their brands in films. State attorneys-general claim their 1998 Settlement [the Master Agreement Settlement] with tobacco companies requires cigarette manufacturers to take any "commercially reasonable" steps to prevent the unauthorized use of their brand names in films. The intent was to prevent the manufacturers from skirting restrictions on cigarette ads.

> *"Major cigarette marketers are making an unexpected new plea to Hollywood: remove references to cigarette brands from films and scripts."*

"It isn't enough for a tobacco company to say, 'We had nothing to do with our brand of cigarettes being in that movie,'" says Michelle Fogliani, deputy attorney general for California, which has support from state authorities in Maryland and elsewhere.

[In early 2004,] at the urging of California's attorney general, R.J. Reynolds Tobacco Holdings Inc. (RJR) asked Sony

Corp.'s Sony Pictures Entertainment to edit its products out of the movie "Mona Lisa Smile." The film prominently showed a Camel ad and a college-age character smoking Winston cigarettes. "You do not have permission to mention or depict our brands in your films," warned RJR lawyer Guy M. Blynn in a Jan. 16, [2004,] letter to the studio.

> *"U.S. trademark laws, as well as the Constitution, provide protection to studies for the 'fair use' of a brand."*

So far, both studios have refused to alter their films. A spokeswoman for Paramount Pictures noted that editing "Twisted" would require a lot of work and the studio refused. Sony said that it supports the creative vision of its filmmakers. "'Mona Lisa Smile' is an accurate depiction of the 1950s, a time when it was common for both men and women to smoke," says Steve Elzer, a Sony spokesman. "We will not alter the film in any way."

No More Tobacco-Hollywood Deals

The behind-the-scenes tussle over cigarette brand identification represents a new chapter in the formerly cozy relationship between Hollywood and the tobacco business. Cigarette marketers once angled to get their brands into movies, often plying studios with free cigarettes. Movie companies, in turn, dangled tantalizing deals in which a film would promote just one brand in exchange for big bucks.

Those days are long gone. Many independent film producers continue to seek movie-ad deals with brands like Newport, Camel and Lucky Strike. But the 1998 lawsuit settlement prohibited any deals in which a major cigarette company would pay for a movie or TV show to plug their brands.

Even so, of the 776 U.S. movies released from 1999 to 2003, roughly 80% included smoking, according to a March report by a tobacco control group at the University of California, San Francisco. Much cinematic cigarette smoking is generic, but California state authorities say there's been a steady display of specific cigarette brands in movies since 1998, particularly in films rated PG-13.

Many in Hollywood are skeptical of such figures. But anti-tobacco activists are stepping up their criticism of film and TV creators, even hinting that the tobacco companies are secretly making product placement deals—although they've offered no evidence of this.

The Debate over Movie Smoking

Whether cigarette plugs in movies will lead more children to smoke is still a subject of heated debate. A study published last June [2003] by Dartmouth Medical School cited "strong evidence" that adolescents who see smoking in films are more likely to try it. Jack Valenti, [former] president of the Motion Picture Association of America, rejected those findings, saying that human behavior is far too complex for researchers to be able to isolate movies as the basis for an adolescent's smoking habit.

"Is Ford going to write letters saying don't use our cars if you're crashing them? Or is Smith & Wesson going to write letters saying don't let bad guys use our guns?" says Vans Stevenson, senior vice president of state legislative affairs for the motion picture trade group.

Either way, cigarette executives emphasize that there's little they can do legally to control the display of cigarette brands in films. U.S. trademark laws, as well as the Constitution, provide protection to studios for the "fair use" of a brand.

"The cigarette-brand owners are saying, 'We don't want our trademarks appearing in your films.' But the movie producers properly respond, 'We have a First Amendment right to show these products,'" says David H. Bernstein, a partner with the New York law firm Debevoise & Plimpton, who isn't directly involved in the dispute.

Tobacco Companies May Change Hollywood's Behavior

But state authorities maintain that the new pressure from tobacco companies may produce a turning point in their year-long campaign to pressure Hollywood to reduce smoking onscreen. If tobacco companies keep hurling complaints at the studios, the studios may ultimately relent, some attorneys-general say. "The people in charge of the movie studios are thought to be responsible people, or they wouldn't be running the studios," says Maryland Attorney General J. Joseph Curran Jr.

Last June [2003], Martin L. Orlowsky, chief executive officer of Loews Corp.'s Lorillard Tobacco Co., scolded Time Warner Inc.'s Warner Bros. for allowing "City by the Sea," a movie it distributed in 2002, to display its Newport cigarettes. "We were quite upset that you would allow one of our branded products to be shown in a major motion picture," Mr. Orlowsky wrote, according to a copy of the letter. "An unauthorized use of our valuable intellectual property may be actionable under the law," he warned.

Warner Bros. said it didn't break any laws, noting that it merely distributed the film, which was made by an independent producer. But in her response to Lorillard, Clara Pope, a lawyer for the studio, promised the cigarette maker that it would "attempt to limit or eliminate such depictions in future motion pictures" it makes.

13

OxyContin® Advertising Misleads Consumers About the Drug's Dangers

Thomas W. Abrams

Thomas W. Abrams is director of the division of drug marketing, advertising, and communications at the Food and Drug Administration (FDA). The FDA is responsible for regulating the production and use of drugs, foods, medical devices, and cosmetics in the United States.

OxyContin® is a painkilling narcotic drug similar to morphine and is intended for people suffering from chronic pain. While it offers benefits to appropriate patients, the drug carries potentially lethal risks and a significant potential for abuse. Recent advertisements for OxyContin® are misleading because they fail to emphasize the serious risks of OxyContin® use, and they encourage prescribing the drug for a wider variety of pain sufferers than the drug is actually intended to treat. Purdue Pharma, OxyContin®'s manufacturer, should cease producing such advertisements and distribute accurate and complete information about the drug to the public.

Editor's note: The following selection is a warning letter addressed to the Purdue Pharma company from Thomas W. Abrams.

Thomas W. Abrams, warning letter, www.fda.org, January 17, 2003.

This Warning Letter (revised) concerns the dissemination of promotional materials for the marketing of [the prescription painkiller] OxyContin® (oxycodone HCl controlled release) Tablets by Purdue Pharma. . . . Specifically, we refer to two journal advertisements for OxyContin that recently appeared in the *Journal of the American Medical Association (JAMA),* one in the October 2, 2002 issue . . . and one in the November 13, 2002 issue. . . .

Your journal advertisements omit and minimize the serious safety risks associated with OxyContin, and promote it for uses beyond which have been proven safe and effective.

> *"Suggesting such a broad use of this drug to treat pain without disclosing the potential for abuse with the drug and the serious, potentially fatal risks associated with its use, is especially egregious and alarming in its potential impact on the public health."*

Specifically, your journal advertisements fail to present in the body of the advertisements any information from the boxed warning in the approved product labeling (PI) for OxyContin regarding the potentially fatal risks associated with the use of OxyContin and the abuse liability of OxyContin, which is a Schedule II controlled substance, and make unsubstantiated efficacy claims promoting the use of OxyContin for pain relief. Your journal advertisements also understate the minimal safety information that is presented.

Your advertisements thus grossly overstate the safety profile of OxyContin by not referring in the body of the advertisements to serious, potentially fatal risks associated with OxyContin, thereby potentially leading to prescribing of the product based on inadequate consideration of risk. In addition, your journal advertisements fail to present in the body of the advertisements critical information regarding limitations on the indicated use of OxyContin, thereby promoting OxyContin for a much broader range of patients with pain than are appropriate for the drug. The combination in these advertisements of suggesting such a broad use of this drug to treat pain without disclosing the potential for abuse with the drug and the serious, potentially fatal risks associated with its use, is especially egregious and alarming in its potential impact on the public health.

The Risks of OxyContin Use

OxyContin was approved on December 12, 1995. Because the drug has a potential for abuse and has risks associated with its use that are serious and potentially fatal, the current PI for OxyContin contains a boxed warning that includes the following important information (emphasis in original):

• OxyContin is an opioid agonist and a Schedule II controlled substance with an abuse liability similar to morphine.

• Oxycodone can be abused in a manner similar to other opioid agonists, legal or illicit. This should be considered when prescribing or dispensing OxyContin in situations where the physician or pharmacist is concerned about an increased risk of misuse, abuse, or diversion.

• OxyContin 80mg and 160mg Tablets ARE FOR USE IN OPIOID-TOLERANT PATIENTS ONLY. These tablet strengths may cause fatal respiratory depression when administered to patients not previously exposed to opioids.

• OxyContin TABLETS ARE TO BE SWALLOWED WHOLE AND ARE NOT TO BE BROKEN, CHEWED, OR CRUSHED. TAKING BROKEN, CHEWED, OR CRUSHED OxyContin TABLETS LEADS TO RAPID RELEASE AND ABSORPTION OF A POTENTIALLY FATAL DOSE OF OXYCODONE. . . .

> *"The body of these ads contains no discussion of the potentially fatal risks associated with the drug and its potential for abuse."*

Promotional materials are misleading if they fail to reveal material facts relating to potential consequences that may result from the use of the drug as recommended or suggested by the materials. Promotional materials are also misleading if they fail to include a balanced presentation of information relating to contraindications, warnings, precautions, and side effects associated with the use of a drug along with the presentation of promotional claims relating to the effectiveness and safety of the drug. Your journal advertisements are misleading because they make prominent claims of effectiveness for pain relief, but omit from the body of the advertisements crucial facts related to the serious, potentially fatal safely risks associated with the use of OxyContin, the potential for OxyContin to be abused, and the limitations on its appropriate indicated use.

OxyContin Ads Omit Risk Information

Specifically, your November [2002] Ad contains a two-page spread picturing a man fishing with a boy and featuring the prominent headline "THERE CAN BE LIFE WITH RELIEF." The words "LIFE WITH RELIEF" are the largest in the advertisement. The ad also features a graphic of two paper medication dosage cups with "8 AM" and "8 PM" next to them. The logo for OxyContin is right below, with the prominent tagline "IT WORKS." Your October [2002] Ad promotes "WHEN IT'S TIME TO CONSIDER Q4-6H OPIOIDS . . . REMEMBER, EFFECTIVE RELIEF TAKES JUST TWO."[1] The claim "REMEMBER, EFFECTIVE RELIEF TAKES JUST TWO" is prominently highlighted in the middle of the ad, surrounded by comparative graphics of dosage cups which show only two dosage cups for OxyContin, as compared to six dosage cups for the other drugs. As with the November Ad, the logo for OxyContin is directly under the graphic of the two dosage cups, with the prominent tagline "IT WORKS." Therefore, the principal message of both advertisements appears to be that OxyContin offers effective pain relief and has convenient dosing.

These ad presentations, however, fail to present in the body of the advertisements critical safety information related to the use of OxyContin needed to balance these broad claims promoting its efficacy for pain relief. Neither one of your ads presents in the body of the advertisements any information from the boxed warning discussing OxyContin's potential for abuse and the related considerations when prescribing the drug. Neither one of your ads presents in the body of the advertisements any information from the boxed warning disclosing that the drug can be fatal if taken by certain patients or under certain conditions. It is particularly disturbing that your November Ad would tout "Life With Relief," yet fail to warn that patients can die from taking OxyContin.

1. "Q4-6H opioids" indicates four to six hours of effectiveness.

These ad presentations are accompanied by a brief summary of the prescribing information for OxyContin, including the boxed warning, and the ads include a reference to the brief summary. However, presenting important risk information in this manner is not in accordance with FDA's prescription drug advertising regulations. . . . The typical physician reviewing an advertisement for a prescription drug would expect the most serious risks associated with the drug to be included in the body of the ad. The body of these ads contains no discussion of the potentially fatal risks associated with the drug and its potential for abuse. Moreover, the expectation that the most relevant risks have been disclosed in the body, rather than the brief summary, of your ads is exacerbated by having a statement in the body of your ads that begins "The most serious risk . . ." implying that what follows is a complete statement of the drug's most serious risks, not that there are other, [more] serious risks to be aware of. Therefore, the language in the body of your ads reinforces the impression that the most serious risks have been disclosed, when in fact they have not.

Ads Understate Safety Information

Your ads not only omit these important risks, but also understate the minimal safety information that you do disclose in the body of the advertisements, thus completely misrepresenting the safety profile of the drug. Your ads state that "The most serious risk with opioids, including OxyContin™, is respiratory depression [breathing difficulties]." This statement suggests that there are no specific safety considerations for OxyContin related to respiratory depression, which is false or misleading and could lead to prescribing of the product based on inadequate consideration of risk. This statement also fails to warn that this risk can be a fatal one. As stated in the boxed warning, OxyContin has two tablet strengths that are for use in opioid-tolerant patients only, because they can cause fatal respiratory depression when administered to patients not previously exposed to opioids. Also, the boxed warning states that OxyContin tablets are to be swallowed whole and not broken, crushed or chewed, because that leads to rapid release and absorption of a potentially fatal dose of OxyContin. It is especially troubling that your ads tout the dosing convenience of OxyContin as a benefit, but fail to warn of these associated serious safety risks that come from its controlled-release formulation.

Your advertisements, in this context, also minimize the most common adverse events associated with OxyContin by describing "Common opioid side effects" rather than side effects and safety risks that have been seen with OxyContin itself. In addition, your advertisements state that "OxyContin is contraindicated in patients with known hypersensitivity to oxycodone, or in any situation where opioids are contraindicated," without giving the specific contraindications noted above. By essentially suggesting that no safety or tolerability issues have been seen specifically with OxyContin, and by implying that OxyContin therapy is not associated with the serious and significant risks outlined above, your advertisements grossly misrepresent the safety profile of OxyContin. This implication is false or misleading and raises significant public health and safety concerns.

Ads Overstate Who Can Take Oxycontin

Your advertisements suggest that OxyContin can be used in a much broader range of pain patients than has been proven to be safe and effective. This is even more problematic from a public health perspective given the serious safety risks associated with the drug and the serious deficiencies in the safety information presented in your advertisements.

The only indication information presented in the body of the advertisements (indeed, the only information from the boxed warning included at all as part of the body of these advertisements) is the partial language from the Indications and Usage section of the PI, "For moderate to severe pain when a continuous, around-the-clock analgesic [pain reliever] is needed for an extended period of time," which you present by itself at the top of these advertisements. In the November Ad, this information is located in the upper left-hand corner of the picture on the first page of the spread, in small white type over a background of green leaves and blue sky. It is also the only writing on that page. This information is not prominent, and is not adequately communicated, especially in contrast to the prominent claim of "THERE CAN BE LIFE WITH RELIEF" and all the other text of the advertisement on the next page. Similarly, in the October Ad, this partial indication language is included at the top of the ad in a much smaller typesize than the prominent claims related to "effective relief" with the drug. These presentations are insufficient to give appropriate context and balance to your claims broadly promoting the use of this drug for pain relief. In addition, in your November Ad, you portray a seemingly healthy, unimpaired man out fishing and taking care of a child, rather than depicting a more typical person with persistent, moderate to severe pain taking OxyContin. Therefore your advertisements fail to adequately communicate the actual indication for OxyContin and suggest its use for pain relief in a much broader range of patients than indicated. . . .

Also of concern, your advertisements, and in particular, your October Ad, represent the dosing convenience of OxyContin by showing dosage cups of the type used to dispense medication in a hospital setting, along with your broad claims of efficacy. The body of the advertisements, however, fails to present the important limitations on the use of OxyContin restricting it to certain hospitalized patients as described in the OxyContin PI. . . .

Addressing the Problem

You have disseminated promotional journal advertisements that fail to disclose in the body of the advertisements serious and significant risks associated with the use of OxyContin and important limitations on the indicated use of the drug.

Because of the significant public health and safety concerns raised by your advertisements, we request that you provide a detailed response to the issues raised in this Warning Letter. This response should contain an action plan that includes:

1. Immediately ceasing the dissemination of these advertisements and all other promotional materials that contain the same or similar violations outlined in this letter.
2. Providing a plan of action to disseminate accurate and complete information to the audience(s) that received the misleading messages.
3. A written statement of your intent to comply with "1" and "2" above. . . .

The violations discussed in this letter do not necessarily constitute an exhaustive list. We are continuing to evaluate other aspects of your promotional campaign for OxyContin, and may determine that additional remedial messages will be necessary to fully correct the false or misleading messages resulting from your violative conduct.

14

OxyContin® Advertising Does Not Mislead Consumers About the Drug's Dangers

Sally Satel

Sally Satel, a psychiatrist, is the W.H. Brady Fellow at the American Enterprise Institute for Public Policy Research. Her articles have appeared in publications such as the New Republic, *the* Wall Street Journal, *and the* New York Times. *She is the author of* PC, M.D.: How Political Correctness Is Corrupting Medicine.

OxyContin® is a pain-relieving drug intended for people with chronic pain. It offers substantial benefits to such patients. However, it also carries serious risks and potential for abuse. The Food and Drug Administration (FDA) has charged the drug's maker, Purdue Pharma, with creating ads for OxyContin® that are misleading because they do not appropriately describe the dangers associated with taking the drug. The FDA's main complaints are the ads' failure to mention potentially fatal risks and the implication that OxyContin® is suitable for a broad range of patients. However, the FDA's complaints are unfounded. Complete risk information can be found in the fine-print section of the ads. Also, doctors are well informed about the risks of drugs such as OxyContin® and the symptoms they are intended to treat; thus, doctors can be trusted to prescribe them appropriately. Oxy-

Contin® ads are not misleading and should not be targeted by the FDA for such censure.

OxyContin, the potent prescription painkiller, is in the spotlight—again. [In 2001] it was news because drug addicts in New England and Appalachia were injecting it to get a heroin-like high. Pharmacies were robbed, drug-rings sprang up, unscrupulous doctors ran pill mills.

Incredibly, the drug's maker, Purdue Pharma, was directly blamed for the intentional abuse of its product. Almost 200 lawsuits were filed by plaintiffs charging the company with over-marketing OxyContin—allegedly leading to its over-prescription by doctors and thus greater chances of getting into the wrong hands. To date, judges have dismissed all cases before them—mainly because the plaintiffs turned out to be already-established abusers of heroin, cocaine or illegally obtained pain pills—but now, thanks to the FDA [Food and Drug Administration] trial lawyers are again circling.

> *"The [OxyContin] ads are for doctors, not patients and certainly not drug abusers."*

In late December [2002], the FDA's Division of Drug Marketing, Advertising and Communications issued a seven-page warning letter to Purdue. "Your journal advertisements omit and minimize the serious safety risks associated with OxyContin and promote it for uses beyond which have been proven safe and effective" charged federal regulators in a letter described by the *Wall Street Journal* as "unusually harsh" and "blistering" by the *Boston Globe.*

OxyContin Is for Patients with Chronic Pain

Before reviewing the FDA's specific anxieties, some background. OxyContin is an opioid drug in the same category as morphine. It is not intended for toothaches and transient post-operative pain; it is for people with searing and prolonged agony due to diseases like cancer, neurological illness, degenerative discs, and deforming rheumatoid arthritis. The name is a contraction of *oxycodone* (the active ingredient in Percocet) and the word *continuous*, referring to its slow release feature. For comparison: the strongest dose of a single Percocet pill contains 10 mg. of oxycodone while OxyContin is available in strengths of up to 80 mg.

> *"Companies are keen to comply with FDA guidelines but such subjective, almost capricious, interpretations by the marketing division can make the task nearly impossible."*

Available since 1995, the medication is now the most prescribed narcotic, in large part because it is taken only twice a day; other narcotic painkillers are taken every three to six hours. The 12-hour controlled delivery keeps blood levels steady, an important feature when pain is constant and severe. Also, the fewer daily peaks in blood level and the slower the rate of increase in blood level—both afforded by regular administration of a time release drug—the lower its addictive potential. The medication is widely praised by patients and physicians for severe, uncompromising pain.

The FDA Charges Against Purdue

Now [in 2003] the FDA is charging Purdue with "false and misleading measures" based on two advertisements that appeared this fall [2002] in the *Journal of the American Medical Association.* The body of the first ad depicts a man fishing with a young boy in a bucolic stream. "There can be life with relief" reads the large print message. The text says, in part: "For moderate to severe pain when a continuous, around-the-clock analgesic is needed for an extended period of time. . . . The most serious risk with opioids, including OxyContin, is respiratory depression." Finally, the ad instructs the reader to consult the package insert text and the "boxed warning," both on the reverse side of the ad.

The second ad carries the same indication and risk information but instead of the fishing men, the ad shows just dispensing cups, comparing the number needed for other painkillers (up to six dosings a day) with only two for OxyContin. . . .

Here are the key objections of the FDA:

1. Failure to mention risks: Fatal risks (of complete respira-

tory depression, bowel paralysis, and potential for abuse) are not mentioned on the illustrated body of the ads. Thus, according to the warning letter, the ad "reinforces the impression that the most serious risks have been disclosed when the fact is they have not." The letter also admonishes Purdue for not warning in the ad's body against breaking, crushing or chewing tablets.

2. Misleading illustration: The regulators claim that the fishing man depicted in the ad is "seemingly healthy, unimpaired . . . and taking care of a child" and so not the "typical person" taking OxyContin. This suggests to doctors reading the ad, FDA insists, that the drug is meant for a "broader range" of patients than is actually appropriate. The dispensing cup visuals are also a problem, regulators say, as they are likely to be interpreted by doctors as indicating that OxyContin is to be used for acute post-operative pain, which it is not.

3. Misleading headline: The FDA says "it is particularly disturbing that your [fishing ad] would tout 'Life with Relief,' yet fail to warn that patients can die from taking OxyContin".

FDA Charges Unfounded

These gripes are plainly absurd.

First, every bit of information that the FDA says is missing from the body of the ad can be found in the fine print section of the ad on the reverse side of the page. The FDA's drug advertising regulation, 21 C.F.R. section 202.1, requires "fair balance" between risks and effectiveness, though does not say precisely what has to be in the body of the ad in every specific. Taken as prescribed by a competent physician, OxyContin actually poses minimal risks (e.g., constipation, nausea, itching) and great potential benefit. Chopped up and snorted or injected—the way it is consumed by addicts, not legitimate pain patients—the medication can indeed lead to overdose and death. But the ads are for doctors, not patients and certainly not drug abusers.

Second, does the FDA think doctors are stupid? We know that opioids have enormous abuse potential and at high doses can lead to respiratory collapse. We learn this by the third year of medical school. In addition, detailed information outlining the menu of possible risks appear on the reverse page. These ads are not direct-to-consumer; they are for doctors. Doctors know that if you crush a time release pill and swallow it, a potentially fatal dose is released. Doctors know that "boxed warnings" need to be taken very seriously.

Third, and more generally, this episode raises the question: what is the standard here? Many of the assumptions made by regulators—that doctors will interpret the fishing men as meaning OxyContin is to be used for mild pain; that dispensing cups signify acute post-op use; that doctors will not read an entire ad or that they have minimal implicit knowledge of opioids—are unfounded and arbitrary. Companies are keen to comply with FDA guidelines but such subjective, almost capricious, interpretations by the marketing division can make the task nearly impossible.

I have no idea what's behind the FDA censure. Surely, the agency could have simply asked Purdue to rearrange the ad text but a warning letter—especially one condemning ads as "egregious and alarming"—exposes the company to liability anew. "This [letter] will go a long way in the courts," said Troy N. Giatras, a Charleston, W. Va. lawyer who heads the Association of Trial Lawyers of America's OxyContin litigation group. "Coming from the FDA, it will have great weight with judges and juries," he told the *Boston Globe* in late January [2003].

Recently, Mark McLellan, a physician and well-regarded policymaker, was appointed FDA commissioner. Among his many stated goals—ironically, perhaps, in light of Purdue's circumstances—is a crack-down on misleading pharmaceutical advertising. Fine, but Dr. McLellan needs to make sure that his people know a misleading ad when they see one. . . . Issuing a groundless and inflammatory warning has consequences that can only undermine the progress the FDA, under new leadership, hopes to make.

Organizations to Contact

The editors have compiled the following list of organizations concerned with the issues debated in this book. The descriptions are derived from materials provided by the organizations. All have publications or information available for interested readers. The list was compiled on the date of publication of the present volume; names, addresses, phone and fax numbers, and e-mail addresses may change. Be aware that many organizations take several weeks or longer to respond to inquiries, so allow as much time as possible.

Adbusters Media Foundation
1243 W. Seventh Ave., Vancouver, BC V6H 1B7 Canada
(604) 736-9401 • fax: (604) 737-6021
e-mail: info@adbusters.org • Web site: www.adbusters.org

Adbusters is a network of artists, activists, writers, and other people who want to build a new social activist movement. The organization publishes *Adbusters* magazine, which explores the ways that commercialism destroys physical and cultural environments. Spoof ads and information on political action are available on the Web site.

Ad Council
261 Madison Ave., 11th Fl., New York, NY 10016
(212) 922-1500 • fax: (212) 922-1676
e-mail: info@adcouncil.org • Web site: www.adcouncil.org

The Ad Council is a nonprofit organization that works with businesses, advertisers, the media, and other nonprofit groups to produce and distribute public service campaigns. The council also conducts research in order to improve the effectiveness of its campaigns. Several research studies can be found on the Web site.

American Council on Science and Health (ACSH)
1995 Broadway, 2nd Fl., New York, NY 10023-5860
(212) 362-7044 • fax: (212) 362-4919
e-mail: acsh@acsh.org • Web site: www.acsh.org

The American Council on Science and Health is a not-for-profit organization of scientists and policy makers concerned with the scientific basis and policy implications of public health–related issues. ACSH hosts public health seminars and press conferences and produces a range of media materials. Press releases, editorials, and other articles on a variety of health issues, including tobacco use, can be found on the Web site.

American Enterprise Institute for Public Policy Research
1150 Seventeenth St. NW, Washington, DC 20036
(202) 862-5800 • fax: (202) 862-7177
Web site: www.aei.org

The American Enterprise Institute for Public Policy Research is dedicated to preserving individual freedoms through research and publication on politics, economics, international affairs, and defense policies. The Web site contains information about the role of advertising in the tobacco, alcohol, and prescription drug industries.

American Legacy Foundation
2030 M St. NW, 6th Fl., Washington, DC 20036
(202) 454-5555 • fax: (202) 454-5599
e-mail: info@americanlegacy.org • Web site: www.americanlegacy.org

Born out of the 1998 Master Settlement Agreement between the states and tobacco companies, the American Legacy Foundation is a public health organization that develops national programs to address the health effects of tobacco use. The foundation aims to empower young people to reject tobacco and to eliminate disparities in access to tobacco prevention and cessation services. The organization's Web site contains access to approximately 6 million tobacco industry documents.

Center for Media Literacy
3101 Ocean Park Blvd., Suite 200, Santa Monica, CA 90405
(310) 581-0260 • fax: (310) 581-0270
e-mail: cml@medialit.org • Web site: www.medialit.org

The Center for Media Literacy is a national educational, leadership, and professional development organization promoting media literacy education as a means of analyzing and evaluating media content. The extensive Web site includes teaching materials and publications.

Center for Science in the Public Interest
1875 Connecticut Ave. NW, Suite 300, Washington, DC 20009
(202) 332-9110 • fax: (202) 265-4954
e-mail: cspi@cspinet.org • Web site: www.cspinet.org

The Center for Science in the Public Interest is a consumer advocacy organization that conducts health- and nutrition-related research and advocacy programs and keeps consumers informed on health-related issues. The "Alcohol Policies Project" area of its Web site provides excellent resources on alcohol advertising and youth health.

Center on Alcohol Marketing and Youth
2233 Wisconsin Ave. NW, Suite 525, Washington, DC 20007
(202) 687-1019
e-mail: info@camy.org • Web site: www.camy.org

Based at Georgetown University, the Center on Alcohol Marketing and Youth focuses attention on the marketing practices of the alcohol industry, in particular those that may cause harm to America's youth. The Web site features numerous reports and fact sheets on alcohol advertising and the consequences of underage drinking, including *Clicking with Kids: Alcohol Marketing and Youth on the Internet* and *Overexposed: Youth a Target of Alcohol Advertising in Magazines*.

Distilled Spirits Council of the United States, Inc.
1250 Eye St. NW, Suite 400, Washington, DC 20005
(202) 628-3544
Web site: www.discus.org

The Distilled Spirits Council of the United States, Inc., is a network of producers and marketers of distilled spirits sold in the United States. The organization supports responsible drinking behaviors, conveys information regarding alcohol consumption and health, and advocates for the interests of the distilled spirits industry. Its Web site contains a code of responsible practices for alcohol advertising and marketing as well as other useful documents.

Federal Trade Commission–Bureau of Consumer Protection
600 Pennsylvania Ave. NW, Washington, DC 20580
(202) 326-2222
Web site: www.ftc.gov/ftc/consumer/home.html

Part of the Federal Trade Commission, the Bureau of Consumer Protection defends consumers against fraudulent or destructive practices. The bureau's Division of Advertising Practices protects people from deceptive advertising by monitoring advertisements for numerous products, including tobacco, alcohol, and over-the-counter drugs. Its Web site contains a wealth of consumer information and media resources.

Heartland Institute
19 South LaSalle St., Suite 903, Chicago, IL 60603
(312) 377-4000
e-mail: think@heartland.org • Web site: www.heartland.org

The Heartland Institute is a nonprofit libertarian organization that promotes personal responsibility. The "Smoker's Lounge" area of its Web site provides a forum for commentary on issues such as smokers' rights, tobacco harm reduction, smoking bans, and underage smoking.

Media Awareness Network
1500 Merivale Rd., 3rd Fl., Ottawa, ON K2E 6Z5
(613) 224-7721 • fax: (613) 224-1958
e-mail: info@media-awareness.ca • Web site: www.media-awareness.ca

The Media Awareness Network is a nonprofit organization that promotes media education and develops media literacy programs. Its Web site explores topics such as marketing to children and stereotyping in advertisements. The Web site also provides information for parents and educators.

National Institute on Drug Abuse (NIDA)
6001 Executive Blvd., Room 5213, Bethesda, MD 20892-9561
(301) 443-1124
e-mail: Information@lists.nida.nih.gov • Web site: www.nida.nih.gov

A division of the National Institutes of Health, the National Institute on Drug Abuse supports scientific research on drug abuse and addiction and works to deliver scientific data to policy makers, health care practitioners, and the American public. NIDA funds the yearly Monitoring the Future survey (found at www.monitoringthefuture.org), a source of important data on drug abuse by young people.

Smoke-Free Movies
UCSF School of Medicine, Box 1390, San Francisco CA 94143-1390
(415) 476-4683
e-mail: movies@medicine.ucsf.edu
Web site: www.smokefreemovies.ucsf.edu

A project of Professor Stanton Glantz at the University of California–San Francisco, Smoke-Free Movies aims to eliminate the placement of tobacco products in American films. Its Web site includes an online action kit, numerous news articles, and powerful print advertisements promoting smoke-free films.

Bibliography

Books

Richard J. Bonnie and Mary O'Connell, eds. *Reducing Underage Drinking: A Collective Responsibility*. Washington, DC: National Academies, 2004.

John E. Calfee *Fear of Persuasion: A New Perspective on Advertising and Regulation*. AEI, 1997.

Laura Egendorf, ed. *Teen Decisions: Smoking*. San Diego, CA: Greenhaven, 2001.

Joseph C. Fisher *Advertising, Alcohol Consumption, and Abuse: A Worldwide Survey*. Westport, CT: Greenwood, 1993.

Hugh High *Does Advertising Increase Smoking? Economics, Free Speech and Advertising Bans*. London: Institute of Economic Affairs, 1999.

Lloyd Johnston, Patrick O'Malley, Jerald Bachman, and John Schulenberg *Monitoring the Future National Results on Adolescent Drug Use: Overview of Key Findings*. NIH publication no. 04-5506. Bethesda, MD: National Institute on Drug Abuse, 2003.

Jean Kilbourne *Deadly Persuasion: Why Women and Girls Must Fight the Addictive Power of Advertising*. New York: Free Press, 1999.

Mike A. Males *Smoked: Why Joe Camel Is Still Smiling*. Monroe, ME: Common Courage, 1999.

Robert M. O'Neil *Alcohol Advertising on the Air: Beyond the Reach of Government?* Washington, DC: Media Institute, 1997.

Donald F. Roberts, Lisa Henriksen, and Peter G. Christenson *Substance Use in Popular Movies and Music*. Washington, DC: Office of National Drug Control Policy, 1999.

Jacob Sullum *For Your Own Good: The Anti-Smoking Crusade and the Tyranny of Public Health*. New York: Free Press, 1998.

James D. Torr, ed. *Current Controversies: Teens and Alcohol*. San Diego, CA: Greenhaven, 2002.

Rivka Weiser *Smoking and Women's Magazines: 2001–2002*. New York: American Council on Science and Health, 2004.

Periodicals

Mike Beirne	"B&W Blends Music, Art, Extensions to Play It *Kool*: Effort Features New Packaging, Flavors, More Urban Culture Ties," *Brandweek*, March 8, 2004.
Allyce Bess	"Lawsuit Targets Alcohol Advertising Aimed at Younger Drinkers," *St. Louis Post-Dispatch*, December 18, 2003.
John E. Calfee	"How Advertising Informs to Our Benefit," *Consumers' Research Magazine*, April 1998.
Center on Alcohol Marketing and Youth	"Television: Alcohol's Vast Ad Land," December 18, 2002, www.camy.org.
Stuart Elliott	"Objections May Scuttle NBC's Plan to Accept Hard Liquor Commercials," *New York Times*, February 12, 2002.
Stephen Fraser	"Smoke Screen: Sweet-Sounding Cigarettes are 'Candy-Flavored Cancer,'" *Current Health*, no. 2, December 2004.
Pradeep P. Gidwani et al.	"Television Viewing and Initiation of Smoking Among Youth," *Pediatrics*, September 2002.
International Center for Alcohol Policies	"Self-Regulation of Beverage Alcohol Advertising," *ICAP Report*, January 2001.
Nat Ives	"Is the Alcohol Industry Pitching Products to Young Audiences? Congress Hears Two Views," *New York Times*, September 10, 2003.
Nat Ives	"Selling Caution or Hedonism in a World of No Smoking," *New York Times*, July 7, 2004.
Kathiann M. Kowalski	"How Tobacco Ads Target Teens," *Current Health*, no. 2, April/May 2002.
Connie Lauerman	"What's Ailing You? In the Mass Marketing of Prescription Drugs, Ad Campaigns Make Women the Prime Target," *Chicago Tribune*, January 28, 2004.
David Lazarus	"Bush Tries to Weaken Tobacco Treaty; Its Controversial Terms Include World Ban on Advertising," *San Francisco Chronicle*, April 30, 2003.
Robert A. Levy	"Liquor and Beer Ads Are Not the Problem," *Chicago Tribune*, December 8, 2003.
Elen Lewis	"Smokescreens and Mirrors: Are Tobacco and Corporate Social Responsibility Mutually Exclusive?" *Brand Strategy*, February 2003.
Kate MacArthur	"Coors Slammed for Targeting Kids; 'Scary Movie' Tie-in Raises Ire of Anti-Alcohol Group," *Advertising Age*, November 3, 2003.
Mark Mazzetti	"Tobacco Is Still Smokin'," *U.S. News & World Report*, April 2, 2001.

Index